IT'S HEALING TIME

FOR THE

BODYMIND OF
BLACK WOMXN

*How to Live a life you love and
Love the life you live!*

TIEN SYDNOR-CAMPBELL, M.S.

Manufactured in the United States of America

ISBN: 978-1-950279-30-2

Library of Congress Control Number: 2020914

CONTENTS

Its Healing Time for the BodyMind of Black Womxn

BOOK REVIEWS

"Tien hit the nail on the head with this one! I mean LITERALLY! What better way to connect to your true inner self, than by starting with the inner-workings of the bodymind?! I had so many 'aha' moments in this book, and I'm sure other readers will too! Wanna get balanced and centered? Read this book!"
- Dr. Zakia Robins-McNeal, 8/10/20

"It's Healing Time For The BodyMind of Black Womxn was a much needed shot of LOVE. As Black Womxn we go through our daily lives making sure everyone & everything is in order--placing ourselves as a footnote in our own stories. Tien is everything you need in a guide--loving, patient, and unyielding in her expectation that Black Womxn take some time and wrap our strong, compassionate arms around ourselves.
- M. Anderson, 7/23/20

"We are all fortunate beneficiaries of Tien's decades of education, training and teaching experiences. It's Healing Time for the BodyMind of the Black Womxn is a culmination of that experience. This workbook asks readers all of the right questions while simultaneously helping them to find some answers. As a lifelong truth seeker, I appreciate how it reveals for readers a narrative that correlates the chakras, diet, life experiences and how it manifests in our mental and physiological self simultaneously. If you are ready for some deep, self-exploration, this is your chance."
- N. Sellers, 8/15/20

DEDICATION

Tien Sydnor-Campbell, M.S.

*I dedicate this book to the most incredible parents
a woman could have asked for.*

*My mom, the late, great Dr. Gail Wyatt Sydnor
(aka "Syd", "Q", "1st name Cindy, last name Rella"
but very rarely, if ever, Gail)
And
Robert Earl Sydnor (aka "Bob", "Syd", "Bobolink" and
everyone's favorite "Uncle Pad").
They both love me without conditions, demonstrated being true to
myself, and following my passions wherever they lead me.
They were my first teachers on everything from how to demonstrate love
to my siblings and family (near and far), and ways to be a wife and mother.
My parents exemplified how to be a good friend and
what being an effective therapist can do for others.*

*The library in my home was filled with books on everything from
African history to esoteric literature on the Rosicrucians and
from fiction / fantasy to psychological theory and practice.
The world was always wide open to me.*

*Now I'm continuing the work that you both taught me to do;
advocate for your community, encourage lifelong learning.
and reach back to teach those who'd like to know.*

I love you both with every fiber of my being.

Finally, I also want to dedicate this book to all of the Disabled, Black Womxn who have needed this book as much as I needed to get it written. There are more of us than we think, and we're the ones we've been waiting for. I hope that you are able to discover as much about yourself as I did writing it, and I hope that it brings you a level of understanding you never thought possible.

ABOUT THE AUTHOR

Tien Sydnor-Campbell, MS, CMT is a medically retired, body-centered psychotherapist and worked as a certified massage therapist for over 25 years. A specialist in recognition that the body and mind are not separate in health/care, Tien's role has been to empower clients in managing bodymind imbalances. In addition to a Masters in Mental Health Counseling concentrating on Allopathic Interventions, counseling certifications were Trauma-informed and Trauma-focused methodologies. Bodywork certifications were in: Neuromuscular Therapy, Craniosacral Balancing, Reflexology, Aromatherapy, and a Reiki Master. She has studied the psychology of the body found in ancient culture healing practices up to the modern-day somatic theories.

Once Tien was diagnosed with Autoimmune Rheumatoid Disease, she used her skills as a lifelong volunteer/advocate to educate the public about the unique stigmas and difficulties that people face in health care (physical & mental/emotional) and in social settings. This work inspired the writing of this urban self-help workbook. Tien is familiar, as a therapist and now as a patient, with the symbiotic nature of optimal wellness against a backdrop of chronic physical and/or mental illness. Tien is a vocal advocate, published author (in non-fiction, research and urban self-help genres), a sometime blogger, and speaker.

Tien lives with her awesome, loving husband of 26 years (Leonard), their two compassionate, young adult children (Tisa and Tue), and her big bark, no-bite Yorkie (OhSo). Tien enjoys reading, bingeing on episodic, onDemand programming, refashioning men's ties and shirts for her brand (MyX'd), making jewelry crafts, painting and most importantly, napping.

Introduction to My Thoughts and Thinking

I have been asked over several years if I have a book that people can use at home. I have been reminded by many, many friends and family that I have a lot of knowledge and information that I should be sharing. I didn't think that I would have enough to say to put in a nonfiction academic-type manual, but it turns out I have plenty to put in a semi-autobiographical, self-help workbook.

Interestingly, I started off my professional career being a body worker/educator for 20+ years. Once I felt that I had that profession pretty well in hand, I became a body-centered psychotherapist for the next 5 years. Then, something happened...early retirement. Not because I had won the State Lottery or Powerball, but because I was given the gift of Autoimmune Rheumatoid Disease. I went from listening to the body with my hands, to listening to the body with my ears, and now I have to listen to my own body more than others. It really all does come full circle, doesn't it?

What I intend to talk about in this workbook is not only my experience with rheumatoid arthritis, but also my experience as a body-centered psychotherapist. I want to talk about all of the problems Black Womxn face, mentally/emotionally/physically. What different things that these problems can mean, what they have meant to me, or what it's meant to those I've worked with as clients. There is something about the fact that you CANNOT separate the Mind from the Body and that has been my guiding principle as a patient and professional. This book is going to spend time on my favorite subject which is more or less *Psychology and Support for the BodyMind.* I am always preaching about the connections and why they can't be separated, and that's why I've written the workbook you're holding now.

I believe that having more information is better than not having any information. The information in this workbook should help you to figure out what your BodyMind has been trying to tell you. Just so you know, this is definitely not the kind of self-help that you want to try using instead of seeking the help of competent, licensed and/or credentialed professionals. I mean that! I believe in seeing professionals as you will see throughout my sharing. I go to them faithfully, Holistic and allopathic alike (aka Complementary and Integrative Health).

This self-awakening workbook is written with Black Womxn in mind. The activities are applicable to anyone who wishes to know how to integrate their knowledge of self into their health care. The reason for this is because 1. I am she and she is me; 2. Black Womxn have been long forgotten in terms of medical and psychological attention to our complaints and; 3. Womxn is spelled with an X because not all womxn are born cis-gendered, but are womxn nonetheless.

It's also worth noting that other writers typically start books, blogs, or posts in this genre with the Root (1st) Chakra and work their way through the 7 Primary Chakras up to the Crown (7th) Chakra. I have chosen to start at the top (7th Chakra) because I think that we, as a part of this capitalist culture, are always up in our collective heads. Some people will start with the end of the book and that's fine too. This workbook is meant to be something that you can go back to again and again, but we are starting at the top!

What I want you to keep in mind as you go through this work/book is my guiding principle *"Our bodies are a source of truth, sometimes the truth hurts and we need help"* and the reason for this guide is to coach you along the journey to *"Live a life you love and Love the life you live"*.

7TH / CROWN CHAKRA

How to Stay Sane while Managing Chronic Pain

I didn't quite know where I would start with this subject, but I think that it's critically important for people with chronic illnesses to deal with the (possible/probable) depression and/or anxiety that happens to us some time or another. Depression affects approximately 3.5 million people in the U.S. As a psychotherapist, I knew that professional help was needed after realizing my own tried and true psychotherapy and bodywork tools weren't helping me enough. I was sinking into a very depressed state, filled with anxiety about what else could go wrong with my body and/or life. I could not depend on my therapist-friends to be an objective voice for me. Plus, I knew there were some things I did not feel comfortable thinking, let alone sharing with even my closest friends. Neither my very close family, nor best friends, had a full picture. I could feel how much they all really and truly love me, but I could also see my weakened state was terrifying. Bless all of their beautiful hearts.

That's the way it is for most people when they experience anxiety, depression or any number of mental health issues. Personally, having more than a few friends to publicly share that they have also needed mental health support over the past few years has been fantastic to witness. Especially when I also see the strength it gives others who have thought that they would/could never ask for mental health assistance. It has been beautiful to witness the support that my friends have received for speaking up and speaking out for one of our greatest human needs;to be seen and heard, as we are, without judgement. I am and have always been a firm believer that everyone needs a therapist. Everyone.

Pain, as many of us with invisible illnesses manage, ain't always visible. That is, unless we are using an external aid like a cane, walker, or wrist/knee braces. There are no measurements for fatigue, anxiety, depression, or even a migraine. Yet and still, we have to manage it.

While reading this workbook, you'll see that I always include information about the different chakras involved in each presenting problem I discuss. That being said, guess which chakra is associated with mental health imbalances? Answer? It's complicated. So, the most impressive fact about the bodymind is that everything is connected. The body's chakras are no different. Mental/emotional imbalances have multiple contributing factors to consider when trying to address small, medium, or big difficulties.

Here is a brief overview of the biggest contributors. The 1st chakra or Root Chakra is the one that sits in the lowest part of the spine. It's associated with the color red and is largely responsible for our adult attitudes toward both, our physical and emotional, safety and security. The energy of the Root Chakra is based on the earth element. It speaks to being grounded in who you are. Depression can be caused by feeling out of place and not belonging 'here'; at your work, in your home, or with society. The next is the 4th or Heart Chakra and it's associated with the color green. It mostly affects our emotional bonds and connections. The energy of the Heart Chakra is associated with the element of air.

A balanced Heart Chakra allows us to experience love, joy, peace and general happiness. If it is out of balance, it contributes to both depression and anxiety. Finally, the most influential is the 7th chakra or Crown Chakra in this exploration of the bodymind. The energy of the Crown Chakra is pure thought. It is beyond the elements and exists on a spiritual plane. The color associated with this chakra is violet and is sometimes represented as a crystal or clear gemstone. The starting point is outside of the body at the very top of your head. The Crown Chakra is our connection to the Divine, Higher Consciousness, whomever or whatever you may believe about the order of the universe and the parts of our brain that we do not understand.

Mental health is thought and taught to be solely residing in the head/brain. Interesting... but that's not actually the case and medicine knows it. How is it not in Anatomy and Physiology texts? I don't know and don't have time to figure all of that out. What I know, for sure, is that doctors will tell you that stress makes every single bodily issue worse. It ends up in cancers and all manner of diseases. Can you cure it by not being stressed, no. Can you help put yourself in a better position mentally and emotionally by decreasing stress, ABSOLUTELY!

So. How in the world can anyone get all of this balanced, on top of being chronically ill and having chronic pain? Well, it's not going to happen overnight. However, I believe that anything is possible. At least to the degree that allows you to have some moments of peace.

My personal combination for balance has been the following: individual therapy, a psychiatrist, antidepressants, group (Mindfulness) therapy, daily meditation, daily affirmations, modified yoga poses, practicing mindfulness, and writing. Has it cured me? Heck no! BUT, I am SO much better than I was. When you're in pain, you really have nothing but time to think about how to deal with it. This workbook will give you few options to deal with almost anything that ails you, using a combination of complementary methods. Catastrophic diagnoses are bad enough without having to deal with the additional problems that go along with them.

Coming up next is a short story with a series of questions that can help you to discover some of what makes you tick. Maybe get some insights into why your reaction to things happens that way. There may even be some self-discovery that you never saw coming. This may or may not be easy for you, however, I'd love for you to figure out what can help you *"Live a life you love and Love the life you live"*.

The 1,000 Lotus Petals of the Black Womxn's BodyMind

There is a reason that 'we are the way we are'. There are contributions from so many different people, places, and events that it's no wonder many of us have no idea, some of us have some idea, and even fewer of us are aware, but haven't figured out how to integrate it all. Suffice it to say that this wellness workbook is to awaken your knowledge of self and understand when seeking professional help is not only advisable, but very necessary.

The intersections that contribute to who we are include: 1.) Physical Wellness and/or Illness History and Influences; 2.) Mental Wellness and/or Illness History and Influence; 3.) Social History and Influences; 4.) Nutritional History and Influences, 5.) Genetic History with Familial and/or Cultural Influences; and 6.) Environmental History from Macro to Micro Influences. In order for you to get a clear picture, this is the first bit of work you will need to consider. Having a complete picture benefits the most important person - you. Go deep and a better understanding can be achieved.

1. Physical history starts with emphasis placed on what you know. What do you know about anatomy & physiology? Basics of movement? Kinesiology?

_____

_____

_____

2. What do you do to take care of your body? What does your family do to take care of their bodies? How did/does it impact your thoughts about yourself?

_____

_____

_____

3. Mental health wellness or illness starts with your history (good, bad and uneventful). Each memory has a cumulative effect on current mental/emotional and physical states. If there have been any history of mental illness, depression, or current events that have caused sleepless nights, etc... Write these things here. Answer this question: What will it take for you to have a healthy mental attitude?

_____

_____

_____

4. Where has the most growth occurred in your life in the past 5 years?

_____

_____

_____

5. What are the areas of your life that could use some additional support?

_____

_____

_____

6. Do you have a preferred mental activity / practice that clears the mind? Does it work?

_____

_____

_____

When you have finished answering these questions, I want you to set them down for a day or two and come back to them. See if there's anything more you'd like to add. This is meant for you to get a grasp on things that may be holding you back from having clear connections to others, as well as your source of 'light' or 'energy'. If there is anything you would tell your sister or best friend to get help with, it's likely time for you to do the same.

What is it about a Black Womxn's BodyMind?

There is a meme somewhere on the interwebs that characterizes one way to look into the minds of womxn. It says imagine having 100 tabs open on the search bar of your computer. To use myself as an example: how many things can I think about, at any given minute? I can say up to maybe around 10. Right now I'm thinking about the following: how am I going to write these thoughts?; will anyone want to read this book?; would this be better as an audiobook?; don't forget to sign up for a new insurance carrier and find out what happened to my last one; why is this person standing so close behind me?; do I look crazy with this wild ponytail?; what in the world is happening to this country!?!?; and then wondering if the book, that two ladies have open next to me, is any good. This doesn't even include the thoughts about family, school, meal planning, resources, completing home projects, making time for meditation and spending quality time on my arts and crafts. Adding anything to this list would appear to be too much for any one person, but I'll bet many womxn can identify with what I've already said.

The Crown Chakra is where all of that #BlackGirlMagic comes from and why there's glitter wherever we have been. It is the #BlackWomxnBrilliance that shows up in professional settings, when we are able to let our light shine and enlighten those around us. It is the ability to walk into a room and command attention by our shine. "It is what it is" as my friend and inspirational entrepreneur Yolanda Owens (Skincare Chef, CEO and Founder of Iwi Fresh) always reminds us.

The power that comes from the 7th Chakra is our connection to the universe. You may know this as a connection to the Allah, Ancestors, Universe, Supreme Being, Goddess, Creator, God, etc... The 7th/Crown Chakra is said to be the space of "pure consciousness." Accessible by lightly touching the area known as the "soft spot" on a baby's skull, or the point where the coronal and sagittal sutures of the skull meet (anatomical location). The Eastern and Western understandings I have in this area come through my experiences in Cranio-Sacral Balancing, Reiki, Therapeutic Touch and Polarity. This Chakra governs the activities of the *hypothalamus, pineal* and *pituitary glands* in the brain. Let's dig a little deeper on that, for a moment, as it's been awhile since high school biology.

The hypothalamus is an almond-sized unit of the forebrain with several functions, but primarily links the nervous system to the endocrine (hormone) system. It acts as an endocrine gland by producing hormones that control: sleep/wake cycles, fatigue, body temperature, thirst and hunger, and some aspects of parenting bonding / attachment behaviors.

The pineal gland is a tiny endocrine gland, the size of a grain of rice, that produces melatonin (a sleep modulating hormone). It was referred to as the "seat of the soul" in the 17th century by Philosopher René Descartes[1]. The pineal gland influences the release of sex hormones and if there is some dysfunction it may show up in the form of hyper/hypo sexual development.

The pituitary is a pea-sized endocrine gland that secretes hormones controlling our energy levels, blood pressure, growth, metabolism, temperature regulation, pain relief and ALL functions of the sex organs including: pregnancy, childbirth, and breastfeeding. Personal secret confession: I have long realized, in my chronic pain states, that sex (orgasms, to be precise) give me a beautiful boost of feel good hormones which naturally help to mediate pain. It also helps me to fall and stay asleep. To sum it up, if you put an almond, a grain of rice, and a pea on a plate, those glands control so much of your day to day existence. These things may be little, but they are mighty.

Here is an example of how the energy of this space could negatively affect you. If you experienced a traumatic labor and delivery of a child, had a difficult abortion, or have a history of molestation, rape etc., those painful memories have both an energetic and cellular imprint. These traumatic memories are evident in physical repulsion to intimacy, painful sex (not attributed to medical diagnosis), or mental inability to remain present during sex to name a few.

Considering what has been covered here, reach into your mind's eye and see if there's anything else that could be a place where your body may have stored some mental/emotional memory. If there is anything there, now is the time to journal about it. If there is something that needs professional attention, know that there is help out there. All of this is for you to better know and understand what makes you tick, and what may be ticking you off, or having a conversation you are clearly not listening to. Please remember to be gentle with yourself.

Nutritional Influence on your Crown's Shine

Not only are you a queen, your body deserves to be treated like one too. Purple foods will help you to keep that inner and outward shine and if you don't believe me, just try a few that you might not have tried before. Dig this, purple fruits and vegetables get their natural, royal badness color from being rich in anthocyanins. That is a plant pigment, which is cool because those anthocyanins have been studied and they may benefit brain health, help to lower inflammation, fight cancer and heart disease. Whoa!

I am not a nutritionist and I don't play one, however, I've come to understand from my Nutritionist friends that these foods come highly recommended. By adding the following to your regular plate, you may help to bring more balance to your Crown Chakra:

- *Purple Cauliflower* is such a pretty plant, but it also has powerful cancer-fighting properties. The purple variety is an excellent source of *vitamin C, fiber, potassium and B vitamins.*

- *Purple Asparagus* might be hard to find but guess what? It still tastes like both the white and green asparagus, and it's loaded with *vitamin C.* Apparently, it also contains anthocyanins and has strong antioxidant scores too.

- *Concord Grapes* are my favorite snack! They have thick deep purple skin and crunchy seeds that are rich in anthocyanins. They also contain *manganese, vitamin K, potassium, certain B vitamins and vitamin C.*

- *Purple Potatoes* look so cute on a plate and have 2 to 4 times the antioxidants of their white counterparts. Now that's purple reign for real. "One study found that people who ate two servings of purple potatoes daily, lowered their diastolic blood pressure by 4.3 percent and the systolic pressure decreased by 3.5 percent, without gaining any weight."[1]

- *Eggplant* has come to have an entirely new meaning in the emoji world, but it gets better. It's also a low-calorie treat that has over a dozen antioxidants and helps to reduce cholesterol levels. Now this eggplant packs a punch!

- *Plums* are another sweet and juicy snack and a great source of *vitamins A and C* that support your immune system. *Dried plums, or prunes,* are full of minerals such as *calcium, magnesium, iron and potassium.*

- *Blueberries* aren't blue, they're purple, so they belong to this lovely group too. Blueberries are a useful source of *vitamin C,* which helps protect cells and aids the absorption of *iron and soluble fibre.*

Now that you have some foods to support your mood, I hope that you take the time to journal what you've eaten and see if it's had an impact on your system. Food journals are a great way to really get a handle on what you've been physically eating. If you are going to journal about your overall intake, I'd like to suggest including anything that you feel like you take-in. It could be anyone or anything that you consume, including social media and deep breathing. Your spirit needs to be fed good stuff. I'm not telling you anything you didn't already know. Think of this as your conscience reminding you to do the right thing. Remember that your bodymind is a unit and if it's been telling you there's a problem, believe it.

When the Weather Makes Everything Worse

It's been a beautiful, thundersnow storm kind of day in PA. Well, at least from what I see looking out of my window, anyway. I lay here, in bed, with aches and pains that increase like clockwork when the weather is going crazy like this. It used to be that I could detect a low pressure system, because that was the ONLY time I got a headache. Nowadays, I feel like a weather barometer! Not only do I suffer from the additional pain that my titanium knees produce, I've got the added benefit of terrible migraines that accompany wet weather. Turns out that dis-ease & BodyMind illness is affected by the weather in many ways. The relationship we have to the weather comes through the Crown Jewel/7th Chakra.

My first introduction to the bodymind and weather came from what I heard as a child. My grandma's bones (especially her elbows & knees) were always telling her when "a storm is coming." I can recall thinking (at age 5 or 6) 'that is just the weirdest thing I've ever heard' and yet, she was always right. We had to turn off the electricity until the storm was over at grandma's too. My dad was the other one whose joints were swollen and aching every time a storm was on its way. Thank goodness we have surge protectors to protect the house these days, but that still doesn't change how the weather affects our BodyMind. My thoughts are along the lines of 'why isn't there a surge protector for our body's yet?'

Consider what is now called Seasonal Affective Disorder (SAD). This is typically treated/diagnosed in the winter months but can come at any time of the year, as I've recently learned. Even as a relatively new diagnosis, humans typically 'feel better' when there's more sunlight. It helps our body to synthesize Vitamin D. Wait a sec, I know what you're thinking. It can be super sunny and warm and my body can still be in pain too... well that's because some dis-eases, like RA, are just mean.

What can we do to help mitigate the effects? Meditation is the most effective way to bring balance to the 7th Chakra. If you can visualize a *white, thousand petal lotus*, opening one petal at a time, that's one type of meditation. I happen to practice mindfulness, mantra, and yoga meditation. There are several types of meditation left to choose from. Take your time and explore the different styles. I would list them here, but I want you to do some research for homework.

If you have a spiritual practice, take the time to see if you're getting what you need out of it. Sometimes we do things because that's what we were taught and not because we appreciate or enjoy them. If there's something you've wanted to try or do, there's no time like the present.

There are also a few yoga asanas that help improve 7th Chakra balance. Lotus, Tree, and Corpse poses being a few that I can do. The other thing that I know works on an energetic frequency is called Reiki. If you've never heard of it before now, it is performed by a Reiki practitioner. You can usually find the name of one in your local holistic health newsletter, website, or community information boards at libraries and local coffee houses. It may not cure what ails you but it will help you to *"Live a life you love and Love the life you live."*

6TH / 3RD EYE CHAKRA

3rd Eye-Light and 6th Chakra In-Sight

Poor policy-making has turned me into an active advocate for Optimal Health and Wellness in everyone's healthcare, but primarily that of the disabled, Black and Brown communities. I have regularly attended the Annual Gathering/Arthritis United Conference and participated in many workshops. The guiding principle is to support and encourage advocacy for equitable treatment in both the doctor's office and in the socio-political spaces. One noteworthy workshop I've attended is a two-part course for our caregivers/loved ones. It's an excellent opportunity afforded to spouses and partners to talk about their partners healthcare concerns, how to advocate for their partners, and how to ensure self-care for the duration.

Another conference that I attend annually is the Annual Summit of the National Black Women's Roundtable. The summit brings together Black Women representatives (officials and advocates) from several member states. It delivers reports from the previous years' progress on political changes and challenges, social and reproductive justice, and promotion of self-care.

One year I was asked to present the Healthy Living and Nutrition session. During the talk, I spoke about the necessity of having different colored foods on your plate and what they mean to your bodymind. We also touched on what each color represents in its association with the seven major chakras. For example, Orange is associated with the Sacral / 2nd chakra and Cancer Prevention. Orange foods contain beta-carotene (Vitamin A) and Vitamin C which supports immune system health, fights harmful free radicals, aids in collagen production, and helps prevent prostate cancer along with many other health benefits. We had a lively discussion about our current plating issues and what we could do to improve our habits. When it was over, the attendees offered their thanks and shared the lessons they learned as a result. THIS is my favourite way to contribute to society. This is my give-back. I accepted that I am a Wellness Advocate through and through. AND, It's mostly because I keep my 3rd-eye open all the time.

The 3rd-eye chakra represents *insight and intuition*. The color associated with it is indigo, a blend of blue and purple/violet. When the 3rd-eye is balanced you are able to **see** the bigger picture. If balanced, it will prevent you from having a myopic view of the world and what's happening around you. Maintaining a balanced third-eye allows you to receive and understand your internal voice/divine **guidance.** This is especially important for those of us with chronic illness when it's time to be an advocate for ourselves or others.

Advocacy may not seem like it's your calling, but we are all here for a purpose. Our 'purpose is an internally guided divine assignment, and we are meant to serve others as we would ourselves and that is with much love. That's my story and I'm sticking to it. Don't worry, I'm not trying to put a picket sign in your hand. However, I am asking you to put *yourself* first, even if advocating seems like a daunting task. If you don't advocate for yourself, who will? You see, serving with love is self-love. That's all I want you to do. And practice, practice, practice.

The Jewel at the 3rd Eye of the Black Womxn's BodyMind
"Every head has its own headache." ~ Arabic proverb

Sometimes our bodymind becomes overloaded and the result is a headache or a migraine. The nature of these headaches and migraines can vary from mental/emotional triggers to physical triggers. A headache is never just a headache in my experience. Understanding them is one of the primary goals of this semi-autobiographical, urban/self-help workbook. Yes, I'm very much aware that headaches and migraines are two different animals. I've had a migraine that's lasted 2.5 days this week, but it started 2 days after having a 2-day headache. Intensity, auras and sensitivities are how I measure the difference.

I think that we are all pretty much aware that stress can cause very severe headaches and 48 hour migraines. I also think that we should *know how to reduce our stress* whenever possible. We've all been told more than once through the news media, family, physicians and others that we should take care of these through meditation, medication, prayer, yoga, mindfulness, etc. Well, I know I have been. The one thing that helps me the most? Listening to my body and all of her messages. Of course I can't stop each and every migraine in its tracks, but I am better able to handle them through simple and effective listening skills. Bear with me.

Did you know that, in energetic philosophies, headaches and some types of migraines are related to imbalances in the 6th chakra aka your 3rd eye? Imbalances are tied together by past experiences and current struggles for control. Mental/emotional imbalances can look like a history of not being able to manage internal conflict, holding onto the past, refusing to acknowledge what you may know or displaying self-control, is evidence of an imbalance. A physical imbalance can be related to trigger points in the muscle tissues, subluxations in the cervical spine, certain overpowering smells/scents and/or food related.

The location of the 3rd-Eye Chakra is in the space between your eyebrows, just a bit above where the brows would meet if they ran into each other. If you are able, the next time your body tells you that a migraine is on its way to you, do this. Take your left hand, place it over your forehead and breathe slowly and deeply for 30 seconds. See if there's a message from your bodymind. Is it telling you to stop/start doing something? Listen and act with an open mind.

Here are some questions for you to consider if you experience frequent headaches. Although similar in location, migraines are another issue as any *migraineur* (self-described term by migraine sufferers) can tell you. As to the BodyMind connection, migraines can come under both the 7th and 6th chakra so apply questions from both sections to help you to discover some possible influences and connections to help manage symptoms.

1. What are you 'looking at' in your mind's eye?

_____

_____

2. Where else might you be feeling this stress in your body?

_____

_____

3. What is your relationship to intuition?

_____

_____

4. What just happened before this migraine reared its head?

_____

_____

Spending just a little bit more time on the 6th chakra: the way to recognize the imbalances is to ask yourself some questions. What is also important is that you clearly and concisely ANSWER those questions. What are these questions I speak of?

5. Do you know how to take care of yourself when a headache or migraine is coming on?

_____

6. Do you actually take the time to DO what works? What does that look like?

_____

7. What kind of support do you have or how can others support you when this happens? If you don't have answers to these questions, this is now your homework. Think about it like this, if you don't know what to do, how will anyone else know what to do for you?

_____

_____

If the problem is the physical eye (e.g., sty, cataracts, glaucoma, poor vision) ask yourself if any of these questions apply:

8. If you are having frequent bouts of dizziness, it is time to see a physician / neurologist.

9. Have you been experiencing extreme nervousness and/or anxiety, seek counseling ASAP.

10. Do you find yourself being overly analytical or filled with anxiety? If so, use your best judgement on professional help.

11. Do you feel as if you've been cut off from your life's purpose? A career counselor might be of help, especially if your work shifted during the Covid19 pandemic.

12. Are you having difficulty falling or staying asleep? A sleep specialist may be necessary.

The questions listed here are just a starting point. It is not exhaustive and it doesn't contain all of the questions that a professional may ask. It is only a guide to help you get used to asking your bodymind questions, and listening to the answers. What I want most for you is to be able to help yourself before, during, or after you understand that something is out of order. Remember, **your body is a source of truth and sometimes the truth hurts**.

I See Eye-Sore Sights, Do You?

I started this year with a fantastic view of things to come. Who's with me? I have done all reflecting that I am going to do with regard to last year and I am looking forward to more RA advocacy work and travel in my life. So, let's talk about looking forward. I want to talk about those beautiful eyes and insights. These beautiful windows to the soul of folks.

How we see things and how we interpret insights vary from day-to-day. I'd like to think that phrases like "I'll believe it when I see it" have their place in conversation, but what I know is that *the eyes can be deceived and that views can be skewed*. Clients have come to me for *insight* as to why their partners don't *see* things the way they do. Teenagers and young adults have worked with me to try and better *see* their parents as people. Employees want to *see* their work validated or goals to fruition. Entrepreneurs want a new view. My physical eyes have been giving me hell since the gift of RA was bestowed upon me. My mental eyes have had more than a few new insights regarding my life.

The eyes are directly reflected in the 6th chakra, and the 3rd-eye is known as the gateway to higher consciousness and perceptions beyond what the physical eye can see. This chakra is known to be the mediator of human enlightenment, precognition, and auras in cultures across the globe. It is depleted during headaches, migraines, visual problems (including not wanting to see the truth of something) and depression. It is strengthened through meditation, affirmation, and specific yoga asanas. You would know that your 3rd-eye is balanced if you're willing to follow your intuition without worry of potential problems that are out of your control anyway.

Apparently, my 3rd-eye and I have an ongoing tug-of-war with some level of insight or intuition issues, because we (me & my eyes) have a history of vision issues getting worse and more dry at the same time. Yes, it's a part of the condition with RA, but I don't like it. So, what I have done is increase meditation and visualization in addition to a few yoga poses for a more balanced 3rd-eye. The ones I can do are prayer position over 3rd-eye, child's pose, downward dog, and seated forward bend.

Since increasing this practice, and I don't have scientific proof, I have experienced fewer debilitating migraines and headaches over the past few months. This is not going to cure blindness or reverse physical damage that already exists, but it IS yet another way to practice *Living a life you love and Loving the life you live.*

Nutritional Influence on 3rd Eye

Much of the food that was listed in the Crown Chakra nutritional additions also apply to the 6th/3rd-eye. For the purposes of this section the 3rd-eye list consists of vitamins, herbs, and spices meant to help support your immune system.

Vitamin B12

Vitamin D3 (cholecalciferol) - is officially a prohormone and not a vitamin; critical to bone development and calcium absorption; 90% comes from exposure to sunlight; 10% from food sources (mainly meat) so that means protect your skin but get some sun!

Lutein - A carotenoid related to beta-carotene and Vit A; Found in *broccoli, grapes, kale, kiwi fruit, spinach, squash, and zucchini.*

Herbs to add to your favorite dishes:

Dill	*Juniper*	*Mugwort*	*Thyme*
Poppy seed.	*Rosemary*	*Valerian*	

Spices to use in preparing your food:

Cardamom	*Mint*	*Sage*
Ginger	*Nutmeg*	*Turmeric*

Infuse 2-3 drops of edible essential oil with your favorite tea:

Clary Sage	*Lavender*	*Spearmint*
Eyebright	*Lemongrass*	*Star Anise*
Jasmine Flower	*Mugwort*	*Passion Flower*

I ain't mad at RA but...

Mental health and chronic illness, like RA, is already a difficult diagnosis to have, without including the toll that it takes on your life. As I've previously mentioned, I was a practicing, body-centered psychotherapist from 2008 until I was encouraged to medically retire in 2013. My specialty was chronic pain management and treating trauma. Believe it or not, that irony is not lost on me. I had designed an entire curriculum to run groups at a clinic for clients with addictions to opioid pain medications. It was all about pain management and addiction. We took a weekly look at natural ways that we could incorporate healthy alternatives while undergoing other counseling and medication management. I'd say that a full 95% of my clients started off as a chronic pain patient who was initially given the medication for pain. Unfortunately, at some point in their treatment, they were cut-off from monitored medication and not given any support or information. Some began to doctor-shop and/or secure similar pills found on the street. Some were exposed to cheap (and illegal) alternatives including heroin and other drugs, which are very dangerous. Very few had, what I would consider, competent care, and even fewer were given information as to what they could do to help manage chronic pain at home. Not even simple things you can do at home like using ice packs or heat to treat musculoskeletal pain.

I was a massage therapist and massage educator for over 15 years, prior to my career evolution. My primary job was to treat pain by using the knowledge and skills in treating chronic pain using complementary and integrative methods. It was this 'expertise' that probably kept me from accepting the changes my body would go through in the initial period of diagnosis and treatment. I had really grand notions that **I would be the first person to figure out how to put an end to the suffering of chronic pain patients forever.** I'm only a little ambitious.

It took me almost two and a half years before accepting the fact that I needed professional, mental health help. You see, I also have several close friends who are Mental Health Counselors, and my father was a clinical psychologist so I had support. It still took me a while to realize I needed my own objective therapist. I can say without a doubt that working with my 1st and 3rd therapists have been fantastic in helping me to manage the dark thoughts that come with all of this chronic pain. My 1st psychiatrist was good, the 2nd was awesome, and the 3rd one treats me as an equal. Sometimes it's great and sometimes I'd rather not think.

I ain't mad at RA, but I sure have disliked the problem of being chronically ill. Getting mad at your illness, disease or disability is okay. The challenges of managing chronic illness and the fear of impending disability causes all sorts of emotions. Anger, frustration and sadness are constant companions when it comes to losing a battle with what you want/need your body to do. However, blaming the disease for changing your life is only helpful up to a point. After that, you have to find the 'thing' you CAN do and do that. If your mental health is already impacted by dis-ease, succumbing to despair doesn't help.

The best thing that I do to improve my mental health and overall wellness is attending a Mindfulness and Meditation Mental Health Support Group. This group reminds me weekly to be mindful, careful, and compassionate toward myself and this physically and emotionally devastating disease. Being around others who are experiencing similar chronic diseases remind me that I am not alone in this struggle. If you aren't able to find one near you, consider starting one.

What I have come to understand through all of the mental/emotional upheaval is that "EveryBODY has a Story". It's up to us to help the professionals understand what works and what doesn't work for our body. Whatever you do to help bring balance to your life, I hope that understanding your body is high on the list of priorities. After all, **it's healing time.**

5TH / THROAT CHAKRA

Tongue Twist and Shout

"I believe we are given two ears and one mouth to listen twice as hard and to speak truthFULLY with the voice we have." ~ TSC

Saying what you mean and meaning what you say can be a tricky thing sometimes. I remember being told that saying the right thing, to the right person, at the right time, is one of the most difficult things to do. Given that there's always something bothering me, it has been a real effort to answer the question "How are you?" with the truth, unless I really want to get into the details. Paying extra attention to the bodymind, while living with chronic illness, requires giving it some extra loving care.

Learning how to vocalize what I believe about wellness and health care for those of us in the *invisible illness* crew is still relatively new. Working diligently on understanding my pain patterns and speaking up more quickly to my care team has been a true learning experience. When first diagnosed I hadn't given much thought to the fact that I verbally acknowledged pain (OUCH!) when alone, but not in the company of others, until I started writing and advocating. Family and friends could see it in my eyes, but I rarely complained when seeing my care team. So, once I vowed to speak up and out to my doctors and not let my forms do the talking for me, I gained my freedom. Being better able to express myself, using my tongue, is a treasured gift. I also believe that the *'pen is mighty'* so, of course, the title had to be 'Tongue Twist & Shout'.

The tongue is associated with the 5th chakra which also governs the jaw, neck, mouth and larynx. It's associated with the color blue. If this chakra is open and aligned you are able to speak, listen, and express yourself from an honorable place. Think about this for a minute. You know how words are in your mind and how sometimes they don't come out of your mouth the way you intended? Or worse, when words slip out of your mouth that might be better left in your head? Speaking without thinking is something that too many of us are guilty of doing.

Keep in mind, speaking the truth doesn't mean you can't be hurtful. Words that aren't used with kindness and/or compassion are an indication that your 5th chakra is unbalanced. Words said with kindness and/or compassion will be received in that manner. This is not me telling you what to say, but it is a call to get your attention. Of all the things that we say, my favorite word to say is "LOVE," and I intentionally infuse my conversations with that sentiment. What are your words? What do you carry in your heart?

According to mindfulness, what we respond to should be from the present moment. Not based on the past, where sadness, anger and regret lay. Not in the future where worry and anxiety rest either.

Additionally, when we respond it ought to be from a non-judgmental place. Have you ever tried to do that? It's harder than it sounds, however, paying attention to our thoughts, behaviors, and emotions is critical to living our truth. In the spirit of effort, let's all try to *be mindful of what we say and how we say it.* It's easy in this day and age to say, text, or tweet the first thing that comes to mind. Remember, everyone else is working on healing themselves in their own way. Take a deep breath and be sure to stay true to you.

The Blue Flame of a Black Womxn's Words

It's fairly well known that when Black Womxn speak it can be powerful. The mighty voice of the ancestors speaks through us when we truly believe in what we say. It is like a force of nature and people will listen if they are inclined to want to learn something. It is only those who don't want to know more, that aren't inclined to pay attention, that can't hear it. There are 2 reasons for the name of this chapter. The first is because the 5th Chakra is blue. The 2nd reason for this title is because **a blue flame is the hottest and most efficient**. Black Womxn are known for being effective and efficient in actions, I want us to be just as strong with our words.

climbs on soapbox

So why are we not believed when we go in to see doctors to the point of more of us dying from preventable problems? This subject is on the table for discussion because we MUST speak up and out. The blue flame of Black Womxn's words should be directed at holding the medical establishment accountable for the increasing mortality rates. The same traditional medical establishment that doesn't have a great history with treating Black Womxn's bodies with care.

All of the advances in medicine have surely helped to keep more of us alive, but too many more of us are dying. We have medicines that can help to reduce blood pressure and medications that help us to live a life that, 50 years ago, would not have seemed possible. Treatments for all kinds of chronic illnesses have made it so that we can live longer and fuller lives. Of course, there's always those awful side effects, but treatment has gotten better over the years. You take the good with the bad, if it means having some quality of life over no life at all. Still, the subject of not having been 'heard' while dealing with medical professionals is something that must change. And we must demand it. If not us, who? If not now, when? We all know what the real problem is because we face it, too. We aren't believed when we ask for help, we aren't heard when we're in pain and we aren't seen when it comes to our lives.

It's hard to believe that the maternal mortality rate for Black Womxn is as high as it is. The top 3 reasons for their deaths are cardiovascular conditions, infection, and hemorrhage. It is that last one, hemorrhage, that I have found to be the most unimaginable. It is also the one that has garnered a great deal of attention to my immediate circles and maybe yours too. Having been made aware of at least 3 deaths due to hemorrhaging by Black Womxn at some of the most prestigious university hospitals in the country has been a blow to my confidence in the care that we are all receiving. Each of those women were all otherwise perfectly healthy, and they all left behind children of various ages. It is frightening. Each one had explicitly complained of bleeding after birth, and each of them were systematically ignored by the health professionals in charge of their care.

I can't even imagine what those rates look like for my Chronically ill and/or Disabled Black SiStars. I can only imagine what kind of dismissive thoughts go into treatment if healthy Black Womxn aren't believed. Where do we go from here? What in the world can we do to make this right? What are the words that we need to use to get the attention that is obviously lacking in many aspects? ***How much blue fire do we need to let out in order to be heard?***

The routine care received by my cohort of Dis/abled Black Womxn includes: multiple doctor visits, tests, procedures and assorted medications taken to ease one aspect of our suffering or another. I see so many similarities in the experience of care. How many doctors has it taken to get to one that actually listens to you and your experience? Not one who listens for ten minutes and proceeds with the care they thought you needed at the start of the visit. The care provider that actually listens to what you say, compares that to what else you have said in other visits, and makes adjustments to the care plan as necessary. How many? For me, it was at least 3 disease care specialists, 4 psychiatrists, 3 eye specialists, 2 or 3 dentists, 2 gastros and 2 podiatrists (neither of which are on my care team).

Attention Care Providers: Is it any wonder that someone could be considered attention-seeking or malingering when all they want is to be heard and recognized? Some of us know and fully understand that our chronic conditions have no cure. We also understand that adjustments can be made to fit our ideal life. It may require that we not take a certain medication because we'd have to give ourselves a shot and can't. Or it may require that we not take the pill form because our gastrointestinal system is already weakened too much. Whatever can be done to make our lives better is what we're after. If it's unrealistic, we get to process and accept it, but don't take choices away from us because you don't have time or don't want to do the paperwork.

Let this be the **blue flame that ignites Black Womxn** to walk into the care provider's office and SAY exactly what we need and ask for all potential solutions. Not demanding anything but the care promised to all patients. We know care providers aren't miracle workers. We still have the right to try and live our lives, for as long as we can, with the help of caring professionals.

This is one aspect of the 5th / Throat Chakra. Your voice. How and/or if you say what needs to be said. When the "cat's got your tongue" or there's a "frog in your throat". When you are left speechless and when or if you know how to speak up for yourself.

Here are some questions that might help your mindfulness practice if you're trying to heal the BodyMind memories and emotions living (energetically or molecular) in your throat:

1. Who do you think you sound most like, in your family (people you grew up with, blood or otherwise) 1.1. What is your favorite thing that they say or do? 1.2. What irritates you the most about that person?

_____

_____

_____

_____

2. When communicating with others, have you been told your tone gets in the way of what you said?

_____

_____

3. Do you have a history of lost relationships due to miscommunication? 3.1. What have you done to ensure that you are listening? 3.2. What have you done to ensure that you were heard correctly? (Sometimes we can sabotage things we didn't mean to.)

_____

_____

_____

4. Do you say exactly what is on your mind? 4.1. Or do you sugarcoat what you say to avoid hurting people's feelings? 4.2. Do you say what's on your mind with care / compassion?

_____

_____

_____

5. Do you break 'your word'? If so, what does it feel like when you do?

_____

_____

This particular set of questions should have given you some insight on how much your *words* mean to you and to those you speak to. Once you have answered these questions, set them down for a day or two and come back to the answers with fresh eyes. Did you come to any new realizations? If so, make note of them and then determine what you want to do about it. This workbook is not for sitting on the shelf. It is meant to challenge what you think and do for yourself. It is my sincere hope that this helps you to find the voice that's been missing and/or find the right way to *say what you want to say*. Your bodymind is ready.

My Voice: The lost and found files

The lost and found files are about finding and using my 'voice'. Backstory: I have been told, most of my adult life, I have a really nice voice. I believe people, but I've been very reluctant to do anything with it. Until now. Well, there was that time I wanted to do voice recordings including reading books, which I might still do. So here I am, in the midst of a chronic disease/illness that will be with me for the rest of my life... and I don't get a say in that. Not to mention that my throat is frequently affected and it sucks.

My personal physical history is that my throat has always been super sensitive. It is also very deep and sexy, when I want it to be. There are times when it's very big and boisterous. I've never been sure if this is due to genetics, being a Taurus, or the contribution of training in oratory speaking and acting. It doesn't really matter. It is what it is.

My throat has always given me clues. Letting me know that I was getting sick because my throat feels scratchy approximately 2-3 days before my head would be filled with a cold. While growing up, anytime I wanted to say something and held it in, the lump in my throat would become unbearable. I would also lose my voice very easily if I talked too much.

Your 5th Chakra is a vehicle for compassionate communication. When you get to speak your truth, and authentically express yourself. It bridges the space between the heart and the mind on both the physical and metaphysical body.

When I asked myself the question *"what can I do to find my voice with this chronic condition?"* the answer came in a few really wonderful ways. The first was my becoming an advocate for arthritis patients. I joined *CreakyJoints,* got some great information, and continue to work with them on arthritis related research. Eventually, I also got involved with the Arthritis Foundation. About two years into the time that I started advocacy work, an opportunity to share my experiences in a book came along, so I also became a contributing author. That book is titled *Living with Rheumatic Diseases* as part of the Real Life Diaries Series. Once the book had been written, I was almost immediately presented with an opportunity to write a blog, which became this workbook. And here you have it! All of these are forms of speaking my truth! How fantastic is that?!?!

Going back to the fact that I've been told to do something with my voice, I was eventually invited to act as a special reporter in the space of advocacy and arthritis patients. I could not have imagined this when I was diagnosed. It has only been a few years since I concluded that, I have, indeed, found my voice. Officially, my claim is that I am an *Advocate, Author, BodyMind Philosopher and Speaker.* If this isn't using my voice for good, I don't know what is.

If you're not managing communication really well, or you know it could use a boost, here are a few painless tips to get you started: 1. Affirmations are awesome. I could put a few in here, but I have a preference that people create their own. If you're not creative, start with "I AM_____" and go from there. 2. Sing! open up that 5th chakra and sing! At the top of your lungs, loud and clear. If that's not your style, you can always hum. 3. Scream! Not at a person, but if you're alone it can be to nothing particular or into a pillow if you'll frighten your neighbors. 4. Stretch the muscles around your mouth by exaggerating the alphabet. Whatever you choose to do, remember that it's just for you and your wonderful self.

Speaking with Ease, Foods for Smooth Talking

When considering the things that come out of our mouths, it's no wonder that our bodies don't close our throats down more often. Communication is a buzzword for health and healing, but not a lot of people consider what we pass through our throats as important. Except I do... and maybe you do too. The 5th chakra is associated with the color blue, as we have already discussed. So let's look at some blue food.

The first thing that comes to my mind is a blueberry, except it's really purple. Don't forget you can freeze them, so when it's out of season you can still get them fresh. Both blackberries and blueberries have antioxidants, vitamins, and fiber which are all good for you. Unless, of course, you have restrictions and can't. Then they are DET's (don't eat that!) My understanding is that liquids to support the 5th chakra include water (pH balanced, fruit infused, coconut and aloe vera), herbal teas, and honey (real only, not the simple syrup versions). Tree fruits like apples, oranges, figs, pears and plums (among many) are also known to be great for supporting this chakra. Can't forget tree nuts like almonds and cashews (please don't try to eat these if you're allergic) which are also supportive and helpful. Whatever you eat to help in your overall wellness, remember that being accountable for your choices is on you. Also, "garbage in, garbage out" goes for all elimination, be gentle with yourself and others.

Living In This Skin

"MY SKIN IS BLACK.
MY ARMS ARE LONG.
MY HAIR IS WOOLLY.
MY BACK IS STRONG"
-NINA SIMONE

This topic popped into my head today as I thought about the problems that Black Womxn face, walking around this earth on a daily basis. Questioned for so many reasons about why our skin is the way it is, as if it needs explanation to anyone. Lighter brown-skinned womxn are asked "what are you mixed with?" so often, by so many, that it's fairly impossible to say that you've never been asked that question if your skin has a lightness in pigmentation. There is always something that folks are afraid of when it comes to our hair. Somebody always has something to say, and sometimes it's other Black Womxn doing all of the talking and complaining.

There are so many reasons a Black Womxn can feel the need to hide from public scrutiny. Black and brown skin is a reminder of the past treatment and current climate of identity politics. Can this skin ever win? We've been blamed for being the object of desire and shamed for having sexuality as *Jezebel*; shamed for being too loud, too opinionated and just 'too much' as *Sapphire*; and framed as the long-suffering, hard-work and sacrificing *Mammy*. These labels never did depict us in any meaningful way. The alternative persona that Gen X wanted to be and then made an effort to combat, and Millennials just refused to take on, is that of the Strong, Black Womxn. There's absolutely nothing wrong with being a Strong, Black Womxn, IF we are allowed to suffer and fail in various ways on more than one day. A Strong, Black Womxn needs to be able to have shortcomings because she's human, even in her superhuman costume. The SBW must be allowed grace, respect and empathy through all the trials of life. Now it's time to ask yourself:

How does the weight of the world's opinion of **your voice** show up in/on your bodymind?

_____

_____

_____

The next time someone tries to lay the weight of the world on your shoulders, tell 'em NO!

4TH / HEART CHAKRA

In sickness and in health, a true love story

What I know for sure is that I am probably the luckiest and most  grateful woman you've ever met. I have an incredible spouse. He has, from the day we got married 26 years ago, been my biggest champion. I had been an athlete for most of my young adult years and fitness was extremely important to me throughout my 30's. He supported my working out first thing in the morning before getting the kids to school and my after work routines. He would get dinner ready for the family and rarely, if ever, complained about doing it. He's always been a much better cook than me anyway, but there have been times I tried to do more cooking. I promise I'm not a lost cause even when he calls me the 'queen of boxed shit'. I still laugh at that terrible nickname. I can still easily enjoy a no-bake cheesecake. Yes, no-bake and yes, enjoy it

The Heart Chakra corresponds to the love you give and the love you receive. Let's talk about love and what that looks like when the

Heart Chakra is balanced. You will find that it's easier to have compassion for others, no matter what they may have done. You will find that you are emotionally balanced, which looks like being able to express anger and frustration and not holding onto the experience longer than necessary. The opposite of this is when the Heart Chakra is imbalanced and emotions are not consistent. It looks like holding onto a perceived wrong that happened months or years ago as if it's still happening. Imbalance can look like not being able to give or receive love easily. Physically the imbalance takes the path from the heart, across the shoulders. It shows up as feeling as if you're carrying the weight of the world or as panic attacks.

Back to the husband. When I first started getting really, really sick, he became a real-life superhero to me. Initially it was not being able to open bottles, having a little difficulty getting in and out of the car, having to take much more time than either of us was used to, and extreme fatigue. Each and every time I went to the emergency room and ended up staying in the hospital for a few days, he was the most attentive spouse you could ask for. In fact, he was so fantastic that the nurses would come in and tell me "your husband is such a great help! Wow. I wish..." He would bring them coffee, donuts, sandwiches, etc... just like he would bring treats in for me. That's the kind of man he is. It is because both he and I have heart chakras that are balanced. We are both able to give and receive love openly.

Fast forward to the point where I could no longer work. I was the higher income earner and this threw our household into a financial, mental and emotional chaos I wouldn't wish on any family. We had two kids in high school and I'm trying to battle a new RA diagnosis, it's a pretty clear picture of the stress that creates. Well, that is if you don't already have that same experience. While there's no competition for who suffers the most, I can't even imagine having little ones while dealing with this mess.

I wish everyone who has chronic illness and/or disease could have the partner I do. For several years while I was adjusting to this new existence he cooked, did laundry, cleaned and took care of me every single day. During that time he sacrificed working full-time and creatively made space to take on part-time, light construction jobs. When I was better able to handle things more independently, he went back to full-time work. We've always lived below our means, but it was still a big challenge for us. It worked because I was able to still have enough love for myself that I could accept it from him. We made it work. Love is an action. If you aren't able to give it to yourself, you won't be able to receive it from others.

Now that I receive SSDI, it has made our lives a bit more comfortable. Enough to not feel the despair that comes with lost work, lost income and bordering on a non-existent sense of purpose. If there's one thing I could say to help people who are hoping for this kind of love in their lives it is this: *They are human and they will make mistakes, but if you can see your way into the love that they have for you, in everything that they do; you will see that you might already have the gift that I do.*

The Emerald Heart of a Black Womxn's BodyMind

The fact of the matter is when our hearts have been hurt, traumatized, broken or betrayed, it's not easy to mend. The heart is the carrier of all the joy and love that you can have for yourself and others. If it's been repeatedly hurt by supposed loved ones, those betrayals become a part of who you are. No one forgets their first real heartbreak. The relationship that you trusted the most with your heart and mind. It could be your parents, a partner, a sibling or anyone that came close enough to the most vulnerable parts of yourself. Lucky for you **it's healing time**.

The 4th/Heart Chakra sits in the space between the higher 3 including the 5th (neck) - 7th (top of head) and lower 3 chakras including 1st (groin) - 3rd (stomach). It represents the connection that we have to our higher selves and others more tangible like family and friends and the communities where we spend most of our time (i.e. family and friend groups, community organizations, work-related business, etc...). The 4th Chakra governs the following body parts: the heart, lungs, diaphragm, circulation, shoulders, arms, hands & fingers. In sacred geometry it is represented by the Flower of Life. It is associated with the color green (consider the old adage *'green with envy')*. The Heart Chakra corresponds to the following attributes: emotional balance, love, joy, music / harmony, compassion and forgiveness.

This series of questions relates to the 4th Chakra and may not require assistance from anyone, unless you have memory lapses or get foggy, like I do. In any case, enlisting the help of *supportive* family and friends is always an option. Answer these questions truthfully, even if it hurts. Continuing your self-discovery transformation process, and understanding the things that may be eating away at your bodymind, require **radical truth telling**. Especially to yourself. This exercise is designed to help you to further identify possible issues from growth and development. Answer the following questions using with the time period in your life between the ages 16 - 20:

1. What is the most significant emotional memory from this age in your life?

_____

_____

2. Is this memory considered a positive or a negative experience? 2.1 Do you feel that this emotional memory is healed, if it was negative?

_____

_____

3. Can you identify the ways that you are wounded from this time?

_____

_____

4. Do you use your old wounds to justify current behaviors? 4.1 Do you ever attempt to control others with your old wounds?

_____

_____

5. Did you have a specific way to manage your emotional states? 5.1 Do you consider them healthy? 5.2 Do you remember when you started to use these methods? (i.e. crying, screaming, ignoring, loud sighing, etc...)

_____

_____

6. Who and/or What have you not forgiven yourself for doing or feeling from this time? Why?

_____

_____

7. Where in your body do you feel strong emotions? 7.1 Have you ever connected bodily pain to an emotional state, especially if the heart was involved?

_____

_____

_____

After you have answered these questions, set them down for a day or two and come back to review the answers and see if there's anything that you'd like to add. I suggest that you take some time to figure out the best way to handle your new discoveries. That could mean practicing Radical Forgiveness™, writing a letter, journaling how you plan to heal any hurts, or how you will act moving forward. Our bodymind was made to love and be loved. Where there is hurt, there is also an opportunity for healing.

Stop Wearing Your Shoulders On Your Head

I took a 2-week vacation from the self-imposed responsibilities of writing. I initially put pressure on myself to get it done at the same time daily, and if not written at the same time, having something done by the end of the week. Apparently, even this proved difficult for me. So I decided to let go of the things that I am trying to do and allow myself to do what I can, when I can. The perfectionist in me could not accept that reality even when I thought I had accepted it. Unnecessary pressure that shows up wherever there is a *path of least resistance.* In this case, the non-acceptance in my mind led straight to increased pain and decreased mobility of my right arm, in addition to tingling in my fingers. It is my dominant side and the arm that I have trusted the most. To do the things I want to do like write, hold a cup of coffee, pick up a bag, or shake a hand. It has been difficult, if not impossible, to do anything I'm accustomed to, with my right arm.

This is not the first time I've had to deal with pain or immobility in this area. It has been the area that most often begins to get stiff if I'm feeling some level of anxiety or anger. Like clockwork, my shoulder starts feeling achy, then tense, and it will go to non-stop chronic pain if I don't deal with the mental/emotional issue I'm grappling with in my bodymind.

As stated previously, the 4th Chakra is responsible for all things related to the heart; passion, giving/receiving love, compassion and caring for yourself and others, etc. Keeping this in mind and what you read in the first paragraph, can you identify my problem? Believe it or not, it doesn't show itself as easily to me until I'm putting it on paper, reflecting on it as a therapist, or preparing for a lecture.

What I have helped to create in my bodymind, in addition to the RA, is more pressure on myself to **give more.** It doesn't matter if it's compassion, care or love. What I feel is the pressure to give more. It's guilt and it's unnecessary. It results in additional pain across my shoulders that I don't like. Once recognized, the trick is to do enough meditation, relaxation, and reflection on my need to control any & everything in my world. I feel out of control much more often than I did pre-illness/diagnosis, but it's always the same issue. Sometimes I have given up and quit and other times I give in to the fact that I don't need to put any additional pressure on myself.

Some lessons are harder to learn than others. It seems that this has been mine since I was made aware that I could give myself more pain than I asked for. My subconscious mind was actively pursuing this craziness?... Seriously. More pain? I signed up for it? What I know for sure, now, is that when I let go I don't have as much intermittent pain. That's in addition to slowing down, drinking some hot tea, and gentle yoga type stretching makes my shoulder feel better. Yes, heat and ice also help that along. Anything that I can do to contribute to less pain in my body is something I'm ready, willing and able to try. Will this work for you? I haven't got a clue. However, I know it's worked for me and I know that it's worked for clients with chronic shoulder pain conditions.

Of course, injuries happen that can cause chronic pain. I figure that a little information about *guilt, holding onto things too tightly or needing to control things is just additional stress that you don't have to put on yourself.* After all, we know that stress is an active ingredient to more suffering no matter how you look at it. That's right, ask your doctor. They'll tell you what I'm saying right now is true. Stress leads to all kinds of suffering. However, managing it is optimally better for you in the long run.

Nutrition: It's Good for Your Heart

The nutritional influence that food has on our emotional and mental wellbeing is really gaining steam in the world of research. There are many discoveries in terms of treating food as an opportunity to aid in healing. There is even a fast developing, new field called Nutritional Psychiatry. Modern medicine has finally started to recognize that what type of *fuel* we feed our bodies has a direct impact on its ability to function. As you might already be aware, sometimes food cravings have more to do with emotional material than they do with nutritional value. Except when you're pregnant. Everything goes out the window when the baby decides what they do and do not want. *I couldn't eat my beloved broccoli for nearly 2 years (pregnancy and breastfeeding).

You might have heard people say that your mood and its correlation to food is new, but so much of what we have in our diets today was not even available in grocery stores 60 years ago. You may crave certain foods that help to alter your mood, like chocolate during or just before menstruating. Some foods, like white sugar and white bread, have the side effect of causing irritability and low energy. When it comes to the Heart Chakra and corresponding organs, the unwelcomed mood associated with it are: a lack of emotional support, feeling emotionally burdened, anxiety and depression. When your heart is happy, you have more energy and are able to handle emotional material more readily.

Here is a starter list of heart healthy foods that can help to bring more balance to your heart chakra. I am frequently self-reminded to tell you that if you're allergic or not allowed to eat these things, do NOT try them on account of my listing them. Get some nutritional advice first! This is just a nudge toward better BodyMind Wellness. We'll start with a list of all things green: ***advocado, apples, broccoli, celery, collard greens, cucumber, kiwi, matcha and green teas, snow and snap peas, green beans, lime, mint, spinach, green tomatoes, kale, parsley and zucchini*** to name just a few. This is not an exhaustive list and what I suggest for homework, if you want to bring better bodymind balance into your life, find the healthy foods that improve your mood and commit to eating them more regularly.

I know it's hard to get some of you meat lovers to think about dishes made primarily with vegetables, but I can tell you one thing; getting a vegetarian cookbook will change your life! I started with one and planned a month of meals. It was the best thing I could have ever done for my bodymind. Remember this is to help you to *"Live a life you love and Love the life you live"*.

The Gift of the Present to the Pain

Initially I was going to write about how much fun I had over the past weekend. I found myself in a different and wonderful space and place with regard to my pain. I was able to attend a function, get rest; and the next day visit not one, but two, museums, even if it was for short (30 minute) periods of time. I was fully able to go through the final day resting comfortably. Chronic pain has been a constant companion but recently, the practice of mindfulness has truly kept me in the present. It has kept me from worrying incessantly about what could happen on a day-to-day basis. It has become a gift to stay in the present moment, especially in managing pain.

Meditation and mindfulness are now firmly integral to my activities of daily living. As I continue to experience new thoughts and feelings about pain, my awareness forces me into a space where I am constantly conscious of the tiniest details of movement. Being able to hold a remote control or a cup of coffee can be a real challenge and each day is not like the day before. Brushing my teeth with ease was a measure I used to see if progress was being made. That is to say, brushing my teeth without causing too much additional pain in my fingers, hands, arms and shoulders. Meditation and mindfulness has helped to mitigate the mental/emotional aspects of physical pain as well.

Before chronic pain, I had no idea that the teeny-tiniest of movements or events could affect my mood. The consciousness and awareness of not using my dominant hand and arm was already a source of serious frustration. Reviewing the findings of the MRI on my shoulder produced high levels of anxiety and brought me to tears. My immediate thought was 'who wants to be one of *those people* needing surgery all the time'? It can be hard to believe that replacing parts of my body that don't work will help me feel better. Putting my mindfulness practice to use with the new information meant I was only held captive, by those thoughts, for about an hour. Staying present allowed me to treat the information as information and nothing more.

Having a good therapist has helped me to truly accept whatever is showing up in my bodymind. Acceptance allows me to continue with plans, while also acknowledging that sometimes this body will say "sit down!" Part of understanding yourself requires time and patience. Staying with the Heart Chakra, we will go over one more aspect. A little more information to add to what you have already learned, so far.

Energetically, the heart chakra sits in the very center of the lower three connecting us to the earth, and the higher 3 connecting us to the energy of others and the spirit world. Our and others' energies are always emanating out and receiving information. This may be something you can easily relate to. You know people whose energy gives good or positive vibes, right? You also know people whose energy has a negative vibe? These energies emanate from the heart chakra. Using the energy of compassion is evident when giving others comfort through hugs (physically wrapping the arms around another). To give others comfort, we might place a hand on the upper back or directly on an injury. It is through the hand that we are able to send the energy of love and compassion to others. Compassion is what we're exploring, or more specifically *how-to do self-compassion*.

An open and balanced heart chakra will allow you to release the past. When you're able to let go of mental/emotional hurts and familiar physical pains, it becomes easier to be in a space of compassion for yourself and others. It is in this space that you are able to approach life with no judgment towards yourself or others. What does that have to do with your body? Everything.

Whether the problem is the shoulder or the wrist, we address it with the same amount of self-compassion. **The recipe:** the first thing to do is to connect with the pain. If you are currently in pain (or have a chronically pained area), gently touch it. Take several deep and slow breaths while focused on that specific area (if you are unable to, have a loved one do this for you in silence). Tap into familiar memories of each moment of burning, stinging, stabbing pain. Ask yourself if you are judging or have judged this pain. Then, forgive yourself for judging that pain. Forgive yourself for whatever accident may have happened to cause the pain; forgive anyone who initially contributed to that pain. Now, in that same area, I want you to place thoughts of compassion and love. Send your body the message that you hear and understand that it's signaling the need to slow down or stop whatever you're doing. Next, promise your bodymind that you will take care of it, to the best of your ability. Don't think that if you do this once, it will work like a Magic Bullet, and never bother you again. This is not a cure! It is simply another way to approach the many different kinds of pain we feel every day. Think of it like brushing your teeth, just because you clean them once doesn't mean they stay clean. Hey, we brush twice a day!

Bringing this exploration of the Heart Chakra to a close doesn't mean that we're done discussing it. Remember that each chakra is integrated with all the others. As we approach the final 3 chakras, keep compassion and love at the forefront of understanding what's discussed here. Pay attention to how you approach the information and practice self-compassion as you do. It's healing time for your bodymind.

3RD / SOLAR PLEXUS CHAKRA

Gut-wrenching might be good for you

One of the things you don't think about, if you don't have a chronic gastrointestinal disorder or dis-ease, is having your first endoscopy and colonoscopy. It's one of those things you don't think about until there's something not working quite right, or you've hit the age where you need to have it looked at under a microscope (or endoscope in this case). I had no idea what was going to happen, but I thought it'd at least be interesting to see pictures from my inners.

My biggest surprise was the difficulty of a liquid diet. As a vegetarian who eats a little bit of food all day long, I thought that the liquid diet and not eating would be a piece of cake...oh how wrong was I on that? I may eat like a bird, but I get *hangry* (hungry + angry) when I haven't eaten after a while. I learned a lot about my relationship to food over those few days of prep before the procedure. But that's not what I want to talk about. I want to talk about several gut-checking things that have to do with the 3rd / Solar Plexus Chakra.

The first thing I asked myself, prior to having both oscopy's, was *why is my stomach bugging me?* My initial thought was that it has to be due to one or more of the medications I take. My second thought was trying to remember when my guts started acting up in the first place. Was it 2 months ago? Has it been 3 or 4 months off and on? The third, fourth and fifth thoughts were the various digestion issues in my family tree. Between my aunts, great aunts, uncles and a few cousins, we all have something that just doesn't want to act right. The kicker is having lost my mother to a very rare cancer in the gut, unfortunately found several years too late. Where was it? The one spot no one looked, of course.

It had been growing for approximately 10 years. Mom had annual check-ups and took all of her recommended medications, right along with nature's remedies. None of it could counteract the cancer that started in her bile duct and spread upwards to cover almost 3/4 of her liver. It was stage 4 when it was finally discovered. Suffice it to say, I'm mildly interested in ensuring that my digestion system is cared for and working properly. You would think that I could let *heredity* be the main reason I was having stomach issues and leave it at that. Well, yes, it definitely contributed to my current state,.but that doesn't fully cover it.

Working directly with the body and facilitating somato-emotional release with clients showed me how the 'issues in the tissues' contribute to outcomes like cancer. Keeping this in mind, the best research always starts with an individual trying to answer complicated questions. As with other chakras, this one is no different.

The stomach and small intestines are organs associated with the Solar Plexus / 3rd Chakra. This energy of this chakra is the core of who you are, including your self-identities, your power and your purpose. If this chakras' energy is depleted, you will act like you are *just doing what you have to in order to get through life.* If this energy is overactive, you will demonstrate your power with *emotional outbursts and act really stressed out.* Sometimes the imbalances are temporary and adjust themselves when a lesson is learned. Sometimes these imbalances are a part of your identity and stay with you wreaking havoc on every relationship you have. This is especially true of the relationship you have with yourself.

Have you ever been told that you are 'too judgmental' or 'too critical'? Have you ever been told that you 'hold on to sh*t too long' or 'forever'? I have always thought of myself as a patient, kind, and considerate person. Maybe I am. Maybe it looks like that to some of my family and friends. I am going to share a major secret... **I will ruminate on things for YEARS!** My mistakes, my failures, my problems, my headaches and my heartaches. All of these thoughts/issues have to go somewhere to survive, and they take the route or path of least resistance to get to the tissues. What tissues? Your glorious guts.

The Reckoning: Bringing this back to me and my adventure in all things oscopy'd. I knew, but didn't really know, how to work on this for myself. I was so busy being an expert, I didn't think about myself until it became a problem. Ever since I was diagnosed with RA, I had been mourning the loss of my former self. My mind, my body and my spirit. You wouldn't know it from talking to me or seeing me in public, but that's how it is with *invisible illnesses*. You can't see what's not working.

My test results concluded that I have a sizable, hiatal hernia. That means my stomach is poking through my esophagus. So yes, there is/was something physically wrong with me. I also recognized that I had a painful, somatic issue as well. What I came to accept: 1. Surgical repair won't happen any time soon (doc still doesn't want to), and 2. This emotional/energetic issue needed the application of emotional labor. What started out as a physical need for medical attention ended up helping me to rebuild my relationship to my self-love and self-acceptance. Let this be the take-away from this story: Just because there's a physical explanation, doesn't mean there's no energetic imbalance. Sometimes it's not about *what you eat, but what's eating you*. The wrenching really helped get my guts right.

The Sunflower in a Black Womxn's Soul

The sunflower has always been my favorite. I grew up next to a man that had giant sunflowers growing in his garden, and every year they would sprout up and stand as tall as 7- 9 feet. I looked at them in wonder every year and would get to occasionally walk through them very carefully. As a tall and lanky girl, I felt a kinship to them. I felt like my face was their face. Right up to the fact that I had family members say that my skin was "yallah", which I hated. Those sunflowers helped me to feel good, and to this day they still do.

How we see ourselves growing up stays with us throughout our lives. Some of what we don't like shows up as a reminder that there are parts of us that we'd like to improve or get over. The 3rd / Solar Plexus Chakra represents the time in your life when you are establishing who you are in relation to others. Your personal identity. It's shaped by your previous experiences of what adults have said to you or about you (parents, grandparents, aunts, uncles, teachers, etc...). "You're such a pretty girl," "That's my baby getting those A's!", "Stop being so...", "You act just like...", "Why are you so hard-headed?" among other things that make you feel either more or less secure about who you are becoming.

Developing your sense of self comes at the period beginning around 1st or 2nd grade up to the 5th or 6th grade. This is the period where you are developing relationships outside of family influences, learning how to care for yourself and your needs. It is a time of discovery and the world becomes more interesting and complex. Youth in puberty begin to explore relationships and their sexualities. Attitudes and behaviors of the adults, who a child may ask questions, has just as great an impact as the answers given.

This part of the process of self-awareness is to study this time period of your life. Sometimes we are walking around with the same problems we had as 10 yr olds and don't know how to move forward in life. We may have an inability to have trust with others because of a hurt that happened in 4th grade. Or we may be feeling insecure about our sexuality because someone teased us saying "you're acting gay," and in order to not deal with the feelings we walk around with an instant prejudice against gay people. Starting with the time period in your life between the ages 6/7 - 11/12; answer the following questions. This series of questions may require assistance from childhood best friends, siblings, or close cousins but most should be easy to answer on your own.

1. What do you recall feeling about yourself and your family support systems and relationships during this time period? 1.2 What is the most significant event related to your development (puberty/ sexuality) that you can recall from this time period?

_____

_____

_____

_____

2. What did you think about your body during this time? 2.2 Were you proud? Were you ashamed?

_____

_____

3. Were you ever made to feel embarrassed by your body? 3.2. Who supported you the most through it?

_____

_____

_____

4. Who do you recall feeling special to? Did you have a special friend that stands out in your memory? 4.2 How did you feel about your relationship then? (remember, you are not looking for the adult perspective on this period)

_____

_____

_____

5. Did any of your relationships (including friends and family) from this time period have a lasting impact on your self-esteem?

_____

_____

_____

6. What do you consider improper sexual behavior? 6.2. What do you consider proper sexual behaviors? 6.3. What sexual behaviors are important to you now?

_____

_____

_____

7. What is the biggest secret that you have not shared with your current partner(s) about your sexuality, sensuality, or fantasies? 7.2. Are you comfortable with your sexuality?

_____

_____

_____

Once you have completed these questions, if something has come up that you consider to be serious and needing support, please get professional help. If you want to talk about this with trusted partners, friends or family around discovering or developing a healthy level of intimacy, maybe it's time to. As we heal ourselves, it is important to support healing around you. This is wonderful for good emotional bonding and building safe boundaries.

What are you feeding your skin? A big, 3rd Chakra issue

The important advocacy work that I do has left me wanting to talk about the relationship between touch and how our bodies need touch for health, wellness and healing. Touch is something that we, quite literally, are born requiring. Touch is when we get to experience direct physical connection to ourselves, others, and everything we encounter during activities of daily living. Sometimes we are sensitive and sometimes we are hardened to the communication of touch. Some of us have disconnected from the world so much that we only inhabit the world through our minds. The headless horseman's head, if you will, because it's easy to forget that sensitivity is experienced in the belly. Think about it. From butterflies to bellyaches, the center of your universe is your gut. Let's talk about the connection to the skin you're living in.

Skin is the largest organ of our body. It is alive! Everything that we experience shows up in or on our skin. Skin issues and perceived imperfections of the bodymind are emotionally about feeling irritation with people, places and experiences. This irritation is indicative of a lack of self-love, self-acceptance and/or self-efficacy. Questions about "Do I love myself... enough?"; "Am I struggling with feeling manipulated or bullied?"; "Do I own my life?"; or "Am I dominating and/or trying to control others?" One dynamic question/statement that I recently learned is: *"What is standing between you and the love you were born with for yourself/your body/your skin?"*

The skin is a function primarily associated with the 3rd chakra. It is the seat of our personal power. It is the home of our developing willpower. The 3rd chakra is also associated with the adrenal glands and the pancreas. Adrenaline or epinephrine (adrenal hormone) and insulin are the stuff of life. Adrenaline plays a major role when we become stressed and a Fight, Flight, Flee or Freeze response is needed. Insulin (digestive enzymes) is also important and if it's not present, digestion halts and shock sets in.

If your 3rd chakra is out of balance it can show up in your relationship to food, digestion and assimilation. It is evident in constipation, obesity and diabetes. When that happens, there are indications seen in skin with acne, dermatitis, eczema and my personal favorite, boils. Boils are anger personified and they can get really big!

What can you do to help yourself? Start with the questions asked a few paragraphs back, close your eyes, answer honestly and look inside yourself to see where the answers might reside in your body. While thinking about the possible answers, take long, deep in the belly, breaths.

_____

_____

_____

Meditation and affirmations are always a great place to start when journeying through the body. If meditation isn't for you, prayer works too. The goal is to accept that your mind will wander, the trick is to NOT judge yourself when you do. If you're willing, trading even one bad habit for a good one, helps. Be patient with yourself. You have only done what you've known to do and that is exactly what you want to change.

Taking care of the skin begins on the inside and ends on the outside. What you feed your skin is just as important. What do I recommend? The most natural resources that you have access to. Your favorite health food stores are filled with products. Happy hunting!!

Nutrients Needed to Optimize Your SOULar Plexus

One thing you can be sure of in life, is that you will think about food every single day. Whether it's what you want to eat, should be eating or could have eaten, it's going to come across your BodyMind. Yes, I said that right. You know full well that you can have pie on your mind and your stomach might be thinking apples. So what do you get? Apple Pie, of course! On a more serious note, if you have had or are currently experiencing disordered eating or body image issues, please take care not to do anything new until you have consulted your healthcare/dietary providers. It is more important to me that you have multiple support systems while also doing what you can do, on your own. Since we aren't just talking about food you eat, maybe there's something in here that can help you to understand some of what may be happening to you.

This section is all about what's eating you and what you're feeding that wonderful and amazing BodyMind. This section is not solely focused on chewed food, though. It is also about food for thought. The mental/emotional side of this is who or what is on your social media news feed and what you put on your timeline. Are they positive messages meant to inspire, empower or uplift you? Does your life nourish your soul? Is it heavy with stereotypes, politics, crime or bad behavior? What are your activities of daily living? Take a moment to clear your mind, then write down at least 10 things that you have been eating & feeding your mind over the past week.

_____

_____

_____

_____

_____

Getting back to chewed food for a moment. What do you eat on a daily basis? Do you start the morning with something that is nutritious and delicious? Do you start by force feeding wheatgrass, because it's healthy...but you don't like it? What about something you ate growing up, and doc says not to eat that, but you go ahead and do it anyway? Again, once you get at least 10 answers, jot those down too. Can you honestly say that you are living a nourished life?

_____

_____

_____

_____

Whatever your relationship to food, let that be the first place you start or improve on feeding yourself more love. It's not enough to eat healthy if you hate it. It is also not enough to want healthy eating habits. Even if you live in a food desert, where your options are minimal, candy is not a meal. Your BodyMind knows this and responds accordingly. Now, write down your ideal relationship to 'feeding and eating'. Think about those things that you have been physically and emotionally ingesting. If the goal is to feel balanced, for instance, then get specific about how that looks, day to day, in your life. We're not talking about a new diet or the latest anything. This is about you. It's Healing Time for your BodyMind.

_____

_____

_____

_____

Next, reflect on the relationship you have with your BodyMind and the one you desire. Remember, these connections cannot be severed. Any physician can tell you that thoughts and feelings are consequential to bodily health. Anyone working in mental health can tell you what happens to the body, also happens to the mind. For those of us with chronic illnesses, depression and/or anxiety is a common companion. We also know that ignoring feelings does real damage to our digestion. These connections are critically important to wellness. As much as our goals, relationships, raising children, having a satisfying work life, etc.

Once you feel comfortable in those reflections, your assignment is: Figure out what you are willing and can do daily to get from where you are to where you want to be. If you don't have any idea about how to get started, it's time to reach out and ask for help. If you're having a hard time figuring out where to start, I highly recommend a LifeCoach which is typically quality help.

Now, it's time to get to the actual food and nutrients we need to support our 3rd Chakra. The coolest part of this chakra is the corresponding colorful foods you get to choose from! Think about the Solar Plexus as the center of your internal universe, because gut biome (digestion) is considered a 2nd brain nowadays.

Consideration of the gut biome has recently appeared in research articles with regard to the overall health. Centering attention on the moods and foods should have you ready to think about the actual food you eat. That being said, there are guidelines published by all kinds of doctors and experts I think having knowledge of the food that helps to balance your 3rd chakra might just come in handy.

Yellow foods that qualify as supporting a healthy BodyMind are the following: My absolute favorite fruit, and I'm SO sorry if you're allergic, but PINEAPPLES are everything. They make my mouth water and my stomach loves it too. Now, the rest are just as important, but they're not my favorite. *Bananas, beans (chickpeas and lentils), butter (in moderation, not slathered on your bread), lemons, yellow and saffron rice, yellow squash, yellow peppers, and sunflower seeds (from the most beautiful flower, yes I'm biased).* Spices include: *yellow curry, cumin, ginger, turmeric and chamomile tea,* the latter of which is great for soothing your soul. *Corn* is yellow and some people believe that it's good for you; I eat it. However, I also know that our stomachs don't always digest it because it shows up in the stool. That being said, if you like, I love it. If not, just leave it alone.

Disclaimer: As with everything in this guide, it is **not** meant to replace the work and advice of your physician. So, if you have to get clearance before trying anything listed here, **do it**. I'm serious. No additional pain = No additional pain. Some of my favorite suggestions for self-care of the Solar Plexus include: Dance (line, free form), Yoga (Vinyasa, Bikram, Restorative), Pilates, and Martial arts (Aikido, Jin Shin Do, Qigong or Tai chi).

What's Living In This Skin

I think about the problems that Black Womxn face walking around this earth on a daily basis. Questioned for so many reasons about why our skin is the way it is as if it requires

> "MY SKIN IS BLACK.
> MY ARMS ARE LONG.
> MY HAIR IS WOOLLY.
> MY BACK IS STRONG."
> -NINA SIMONE

explanation to anyone. Lighter skinned, Black Womxn are asked "what are you mixed with?" so often, by so many, that it's fairly impossible to say that you've never been asked that question if your skin has a lightness in pigmentation. The latest attack has come from the White House occupant and it has really become the sujet du jour in national politics.

There are so many reasons for Black Womxn to feel the need to hide themselves from public scrutiny. Black and brown skin is a reminder of the past treatment and current climate in identity politics. Can this skin win? Blamed for being the object of desire and framed for having sexuality as Jezebel; shamed for being too loud, too opinionated and just 'too much' as Sapphire; and named as the long-suffering, hard-work and sacrificing Mammy. These labels do nothing for the collective. The alternative persona that Gen X has made an effort to combat and Millenials refuse to take on is that of the Strong, Black Womxn.

There's nothing wrong with being a Strong, Black Womxn, IF they are allowed to suffer or fail, in some way, any day. A Strong, Black Womxn needs to be able to have shortcomings because she is human, even in her superhuman costume. The SBW must be allowed grace, respect and empathy through all the trials of life. This includes the kitchen, whose domain in the more "traditional" Black family has been run by the womxn of the house. What we learn to eat and want to eat has a lot to do with what was fed to us as children. Unfortunately, it has been based on what is available to eat or make a meal from. There are so many problems in the world and one of them is hunger. While we're not going to try and save the world, we are going to do some things that may help us to *live a life we love*.

2ND / SACRAL CHAKRA

The hidden side of sexuality
w/ Autoimmune Rheumatoid Disease

I was diagnosed a few months after turning 40 and having completed a sprint triathlon (SheRox). I had been married for 16 or 17 years, at that time, and had an active sex life and drive due to the combination of hormones and exercise. But when I got hit with RA, it walloped me! I couldn't even bathe myself for a long time! Over time I noticed myself acting like my life was over; I was sure that my body was betraying everything about the vibrant woman I had been. Bent over to a 45° angle, walking like I was 100yrs old, and a diagnosis of brittle bones definitely impacted my sex life. It became really concerning for me and my husband. For one, I didn't feel 'sexy' anymore. I saw my developing deformities as ugly and my pain as prohibiting me from enjoying my life. Medications had a cumulative effect as well. Can't blame just 1, because I take 14 pills/day, not including methotrexate dose (10 pills) day once/week.

What I didn't know I felt like I lost my sexual citizenship. Gone. I wanted to talk to my doctor, but it never felt like it was something I could/should talk about due to severe activity level of disease. I wanted to talk to my psychiatrist and my therapist but again, it never seemed like the right time to talk about how it was affecting me. Looking for online support didn't really give me what I was looking for either. So I'm here to tell you that you are not alone trying to figure out what works takes time, constant communication, and willingness to be vulnerable. The rewards outweigh the discomfort. Those feel-good hormones that get released from an orgasm feel so awesome AND they help mediate pain. I know right?!? Go figure.

Don't accept feeling marginalized. **Speak up and out** when you need help **because folks can't help if you don't tell anyone you need it**. I know full well that there are many perceptions about what people consider 'sexy,' and none of it looks like a person that has a disability (invisible or visible). There is a real lack of professional and social education, information, and thinking that if you don't fit into the 'sexy' portrayed on TV, social media and storefront mannequins. If it's there, you're either asexual or in some way deviant due to looking or acting whatever 'different' appears to be. Take it upon yourself to Live a Life you Love with no apologies and Love the Life you Live to the fullest.

The Orange Sacrum of the Black Womxn's BodyMind

Keeping in mind the areas of the body that are governed by the Sacral Chakra includes:

- The genitals/reproductive system, which includes all of the hormones that your body needs to do what it has to do.
- The pelvic bowl, which contains the bladder and urinary tract, kidneys, and the spleen.
- The lumbar spine, lower abdomen, as well as the circulatory system, which governs blood and urine flow.

This also includes the mental and emotional imbalances, including any painful emotional memories around creativity (and whether it was stifled or supported in your youth); staying fluid with changes in life; issues with intimacy related to family of origin and especially the sexual partners that we choose; the force that pleasure plays in your life and how you engage in pleasurable experiences. Do you accept them or feel guilty about feeling pleasure? This pleasure does not solely mean sexual, but it does include sexuality. Sometimes it's the discovery of hidden sexuality that makes the biggest difference as women age and begin to understand their wants and needs more acutely.

Continuing your discovery process and adding further study of any mental/emotional connections created in your bodymind, consider starting with the time period in your life between the ages of 3 to 6. While answering the following questions, you may require help from parents/guardians or older members of your family.

1. What was your home (or primary) environment like during this time?

_____

_____

_____

2. What type of support do you feel from your parents / caregivers / community? Did you feel like you were fully supported at that age?

_____

_____

_____

3. How do you experience mental / emotional support? Physical support? Spiritual support?

_____

_____

_____

4. What are some of the things you did in childhood that you still do as an adult? Do you have any judgement about those things?

_____

_____

_____

5. Are you able to stand up for yourself? Are you emotional about it?

_____

_____

_____

6. Are you able to walk away from people, places, and things that are bad for you? If not, why? If so, when did you learn and who taught you?

_____

_____

_____

7. Where and / or when are you most comfortable? Are you able to enjoy that space / time? If so, for how long?

_____

_____

_____

8. Did you do activities because you were told to or because you desired to do them?

_____

_____

_____

I hope that once you have answered these questions for yourself, that you can begin to see a pattern emerge. If not a pattern, something that needs to be addressed. Set this exercise aside for a few days, meditate on your answers, and then take a look at what might have come up. Using any of the methods that I've mentioned, as well as any that you have learned.

Some of the following yoga poses specifically support the health of the Sacral (2nd) Chakra: Forward bend (seated and wide-legged forward bend), Goddess, Warrior I, II and Reverse Warrior. I am sure that there are more, but these are the ones that I can do. If you are able, try it. If not, taking a pass on this is not a problem. The important thing is that you can see the BodyMind connections more easily and you know some things that you can do to help.

I Didn't Order Guilty Feeling Jelly on Wrecked Joint Toast

Those of us with chronic illnesses requiring joint replacement surgery, understand how guilt can play a special role in how we feel about ourselves. The issue that I want to concentrate on today is about the thin line between needing attention and attention-seeking. You only talk about needing a joint replacement surgery because it's not working, right? Those of us looking at more than one or two surgeries get to deal with a host of feelings and emotions attached to our #ChronicPain and need for working joints. Some of us get it in childhood, others as adults. Either way, there are days where it just sucks. Guilt is a useless emotion when managing a #ChronicLife... but guilt can be a constant companion when you need help with things you used to, or would rather do, alone.

How'd we get that guilty feeling anyway? I certainly didn't ask for it. AND it's not always subtle, but it certainly likes to show up. It can happen anywhere in the process; from addressing the pain to the approval of an MRI, to pre-surgery and/or post-surgery appointments, and ending with physical therapy. It's impossible to ignore the feeling of being "needy". Needing help, needing time and needing attention are very real... but do they have to reveal our vulnerability too?!?! Needing a meal is real. Needing help is human. Needing love is our spirit joy. We would die without it. Where is this coming from? What can be done to make it easier?

Look at the 2nd / Sacral Chakra for a few clues. The 2nd chakra is characterized as orange in color, located 3 inches below the navel and is essential to developing flexibility in thoughts and emotions throughout life. The 2nd chakra is connections, relationships, and relating to others in the world around us. You wouldn't believe it if I hadn't already made the connection, but guess what the 2nd chakra governs in the body? Joint problems! There are other areas such as the low back, reproductive ovaries, and testes. Can you see where this is going?

If the 2nd chakra is balanced, you have nurturing relationships. This is extremely important in the healing process. People are hardwired to be motivated by pleasure. According to Caroline Myss, it is the life force behind all of our senses and how we interpret the world. It is home to giving and receiving pleasure. When offered pleasure, even in the name of health or wellness, it can be received as somehow bad. It could be fear of dependence or co-dependence for access to pleasure. Either way, let's not keep doing this.

How can we help ourselves? Any work on the BodyMind requires attention to both. *The body heals with play, the mind heals with laughter, and the spirit heals with joy.* Affirmations are always helpful when said with sincerity. Yoga poses that open the sacral chakra are also an excellent addition to self-care. What I believe works and happens to be my favorite is having a laughter-filled relationship with myself! Also, I happen to understand the healing attributes of aromatherapy. Orange, Neroli, and Clary Sage are very useful in balancing the Sacral Chakra.

How do I know this works? I'm looking at another joint replacement and it hit me hard. The main thing to remember is, by doing what you can to better understand, it's okay to need help. It is okay to be vulnerable. AND, being judgmental about how you heal will do you NO good. Try to laugh at least 3 times a day for the next week and write down how that feels.

Orange-you Glad to Eat These

Current political atmosphere is contributing to a greater understanding of what it feels like to be a woman of color in the United States today. The old guards' desire to shape the country into what it used to be (rich, old white men rule everything) and make everyone else feel unwelcome based on their gender and their heritage is terrifying. Telling Black Womxn to 'go back to' anywhere is the ultimate attempt to slap us in the face. What this country has now is a whole bunch of #BlackGirlMagic and #BlackWomanBrilliance that refuses to step to the side and shrink themselves so as not to be seen or heard. Strength that has not been widely or publicly available has been showing up in spaces that many of us thought we might never be.

> The second chakra awakens and we learn the bonds of friendship, love grows to include "outsiders." We express love through sharing with and caring for others to whom we are not connected through blood.
>
> Caroline Myss

My personal opinion is that more rapid changes occurred when Michelle Obama became the First Lady. She exemplified everything that Black Womxn have seen in themselves, but felt they had to wait until someone gave them permission to just be our naturally great selves. To speak up in spaces where we have been quiet. To wear clothes that represent our difference in styles. To wear our natural, wavy, curly, or tight coils however we want to. To have our hair relaxed because it's what we want to do, not because HR made us do it to keep our jobs. African fabrics made into traditional suits and office attire. Formal clothes for what could be described as African-American royalty in high fashion.

Speaking of First Lady Michelle Obama, she was the one who decided to make nutritious food for children her top priority. Michelle understands the importance of good food that helps the mind to be healthy, strong and ready to learn. Junk food is one of those things that has not been good for any child, let alone Black children. One thing that we can recognize as Black people, is the level of importance that is placed on a child 'looking their best'. This is not meant to tear down anything about how well a child is dressed. However, when placed in importance next to eating fresh fruits and vegetables daily, neither the government nor the local retailers care, so we have to. But. Instead of trying to start with the kids, we're going to start with YOU. So, what is it that you need to "fill yourself up" instead of trying to do it with other people?

Let's explore all of the orange foods first. As always, if these aren't safe for you to eat, please don't try it again on account of this book. That being said, nutritionists pretty much agree that the following foods are good for you: *apricots, carrots, mangoes, oranges, orange peppers, peaches, pumpkin and sweet potatoes. Fish rich in Omega-3s, such as wild caught salmon, mackerel, ocean trout and sea bass. Seafood, such as oysters and shrimp, also correspond to the sacral chakra and probably the reason they may be considered an aphrodisiac.*

Nuts (almonds and walnuts) and seeds (flax, hemp, pumpkin and sesame) also provide additional fatty Omega-3s, which aid in cardiovascular health and reduce inflammation. If you like it, *coconut* is also supposed to be great. Personally I don't like it, but it is supposed to be good for you. Remember, this is not meant to be exhaustive, it's a guide. It won't cure anything, but it just might help you *"Live a life you love and Love the life you live."*

The Reluctant Advocate

This vignette is unlike the others that I have written. I've finally been ruminating long enough that I'm ready to share my thoughts. This time, I'm speaking without fear of reprisal from any and every one I thought I was afraid of for any reason or no reason at all.

Some people may see or have seen me as a vocal advocate for patients managing wellness in spite of having rheumatoid arthritis; patients who have become disabled due to chronic illnesses & patients who suffer from invisible illnesses. I didn't start off that way. In fact, I was, and still am, sometimes a reluctant advocate.

First things first. It has to be said that coming into accepting chronic illness is difficult by itself. There is a period when you think 'I can still go to work,' attend social events, tend to family, and whatever life can toss my way. Then there's the period of acceptance that you have new limits and some things become less important. Then there's realizing that everyone else is learning to accept your new limits too.

This last batch though. I want to talk about them in particular. These folks would like for you to, at least, look more sick. They say *"I wish I could stay home and sleep all day"* or *"but you look so good."* It is unimaginable that you would want to enjoy life. Especially if, after all, you are no longer working. The value that is placed on your busy-ness or business seems to disappear the moment that you accept being disabled. What this means is that you now can be placed in the category of 'being a burden on society' or a 'drag on the social safety net'. Either way, if you're one of these people, it's time to check your own value. Those who need the safety net, I hear you! I'm with you and I am you.

If you need to apply for Social Security Disability Insurance and have to wait 3+ years to get approved, you understand the importance of keeping a low profile. A short story on insurance: short-term disability denied my coverage because my company tried to be slick and send it to the new company, and long-term disability denied coverage (after being physically unable to work 7 months) without any of my insured income.

Why? Because I had the audacity to have enough meds, a good day, and felt like trying to walk for a charity like I did prior to diagnosis. I walked that 5K for a dear friends charity, at more than twice my normal pace and ended up in bed, hurting like hell, for 3 days. The insurance company decided that if I'm well enough to do that, I'm not disabled.

Unfortunately, invisible illnesses like RA don't look like the others, but can be just as devastating. Equally pained are those who continue to work and try to keep an illness a secret. If you're disabled and looking for a new job you don't want to scare HR with special accommodation requests. It's a sure fire way to not being hired as many of my cohort have explained to me. This is where it will take the efforts of the abled to ensure the rights of the dis-abled are not trampled on. Even the advocates need someone to advocate for them.

THESE are just a few reasons why some people hide. There are so many ramifications to delicate health issues. Speaking out can have consequences. Now that I know and understand my disease, I haven't been able to stop talking. There hasn't been a research project or event I haven't tried to join. Advocacy takes me places I hadn't thought to go. Its introduced me to people I may have never met and a part of projects I couldn't have imagined. Balancing the Sacral Chakra has helped me to find pleasure in so many parts of my life. I enjoy my creativity and take pleasure in eating the foods that feel good to me and for me. Advocating helped to bring it out on a national level. No matter what, I'm totally *Living a life I love and Loving the life I'm living!*

1st / Root Chakra

The Ties that Family and Money Binds

Over the past 3 weeks I completed a 21-day abundance meditation challenge. This exercise proved to be extremely enlightening when it came to attitudes about money, luxury, abundance, and how I (we) had inherited a few beliefs that did not match what is wanted for our lives. Some of these things that we get from our family are genetic, it comes from the experiences of our foremothers and forefathers who likely did not have excess money to spend on non-essential things. If you had family members that were able to own land and businesses in the years of Reconstruction and Jim Crow, there was a value put on the ability to save money and spend it wisely. Most of us had some ancestors that struggled, but somehow they were always able to make something out of nothing.

My father's side of the family consists of eight boys and somehow my grandmother and grandfather were able to feed all of them, in addition to other families that needed help. This side of my family, in addition to all 8 of them going to college, all also managed to serve in the U.S. military. While my dad was the only one to see active combat (in Vietnam), each and every one of my uncles served with distinction. There were very few essential tasks coming up on that side of the family and one was to get married and have children and the other was to make your family proud. To this day, each one of my uncles is/was considered a leader in their respective communities.

On my mother's side, my great grandfather owned more than 80 acres of land and owned the community General Store, where everyone could come to buy their necessities. On this side of my family there was an emphasis placed on higher education and teaching. My grandmother was a one-room schoolhouse teacher, until desegregation put her in the position of head librarian. Each one of my aunts (mom's 3 sisters) obtained at least a master's degree, if not the doctoral degree, because that was considered the key to true freedom. There was always a consideration that money was available to buy things that we needed and some of what was wanted, but there was never any respect for anyone who spent money on extravagance. Unless, of course, it was related to international travel; which was very necessary for our personal and professional growth, and definitely an essential thing to spend money on.

These are the types of stories related to the Root / 1st Chakra. The 1st chakra is responsible for your family connections at the roots and the branches that you have created with your own family. It is your connection to the earth that contributes to your ability to "stay grounded" whenever chaos surrounds you. The 1st Chakra, although discussed in the last chapter of this workbook, is the foundation on which all other chakra's stand. This is the chakra responsible for your initial connections to feeling safe and secure in your family and community.

The parts of the body connected to the Root Chakra include: the coccyx (the tiny triangle shaped bone at the tail end of the spinal column); the perineum (space between the genitals and the anus); the hips, thighs, legs and feet. Some of the physical problems associated with a Root Chakra imbalance will be chronic pain and/or illness, in any of those areas previously described. Additionally, gonadal issues (prostate / ovaries), sciatica and restless or weakened legs, as well as bladder problems (weak or overactive), constipation/diarrhea, and kidney stones to name a few.

The mental/emotional strengths that you display, when the 1st Chakra is balanced, is one of confidence, security, a sense of peace and freedom from worries. In order to keep the Root Chakra in mental/emotional balance, the following affirmations should be considered: "I am grounded"; "I am trustworthy and trusting"; "I am safe and supported" and; "I accept that abundance is within my body, mind and spirit." Creating your own is even better, but using these as a starting point is appropriate. It is the INTENTION that is the most important aspect of the affirmations.

Mental/Emotional imbalances in the Root Chakra are visible in those who are restless and don't know what to do with themselves. There is typically a problem with "walking into the future" with relationships, where or what kind of work is wanted, and/or where to live (i.e put down roots). Other imbalances include insecure attachments to loved ones, short attention span/impatience, and being quick to accuse others of greed when, in fact, it is likely your own issues with greed being projected.

To sum this up; if you have deficient Root Chakra energy, you will be more prone to issues such as anxiety around lack, suspicion, and withdrawing from family. On the other hand, if you have excessive Root Chakra energy you will be prone to overworking and greed.

So what can we do about this? The first thing that I would recommend is getting yourself grounded. Naturally, connecting with Mother Earth in all her forms is helpful, but starting with the self is critical. TAKE A DEEP BREATH! Okay, now do it again. Don't worry, I'll wait. Now, one more time. This is the first and best thing that you can do when making decisions related to abundance (of time, money and/or love). Before the splurge, take several deep breaths. Don't avoid checking account balances, be brave, take a deep breath and check it anyway. Don't avoid hard conversations, take several deep breaths and start with the words coming from the heart (not the hurt). Stop and smell the flowers, better yet, take a deep breath and buy the fresh flowers. Take the walk in fresh air. If you can't walk outside, open all the windows to let in fresh air. No matter what you do, remember to *"Live a life you love and Love the life you live!"*

A Trip Back to Red Roots of the BodyMind

Considering what Black Womxn have experienced for the past 500 years in America, it is no wonder that acknowledging traumas has not been attempted by traditional medicine or psychotherapy. It has been the 'fringe' doctors, naturopaths, psychologists and healers who have tried to untangle the roots of our collective pain. Thanking Dr. Sebi, Queen Afua (Heal Thyself for Health and Longevity), Dr. Llaila O. Africa (African Holistic Health), Dr. Joy DeGruy (Post-Traumatic Slave Syndrome), Iyanla Vanzant, and countless other healers who have guided this work is important, but the work is not nearly done. If we are to heal this nation and the world, Black Womxn must heal themselves.

Combining some of what I have learned in the nooks and crannies of books, articles, lectures, conversations and education resulted in this workbook. We are a nation who continues to strive for our personal freedom from our trauma, both macro and micro. This version is meant for you to see yourself in the stories and the growth.

The following questions have been created for you to learn more about your beginnings for yourself, not just because you are trying to avoid making mistakes or wanting to know why you don't feel loved. Looking back, go to the earliest age you recall. If you aren't able to go back farther than age 6, don't worry, there may be things you don't need to remember. That should be something that you do with a trained therapist or other professional.

1. How did your parents meet?

_____

2. When did they become a couple in relation to your birth? If they were not a couple, what were the circumstances around the pregnancy and your birth?

_____

_____

3. Did your parents fight or break up at all during the pregnancy?

    Y   N   N/A

4. What are your earliest memories in your home? Would you characterize these memories as significant?

_____

_____

5. How were you characterized by your parents between birth and 5 or 6? (happy, sad, quiet, shy, hyper?) Would you agree with that characterization?

_____

_____

6. How do your parents characterize the attention paid to you? How do they say you asked for attention? Did you feel that your parents paid attention to you and your needs?

_____

_____

7. Did any significant events occur during the first 5 years of your life? If so, can you recall anything about that / those events?

_____

_____

8. How did you react to negative information?

_____

_____

9. Do you ever tell half-truths to yourself? Are you typically more critical of yourself than others?

_____

_____

When you have answered these questions, it will be advisable for you to do some reflection on how these answers are reflected in your relationships to family members, money, other intimate relationships and especially yourself. If there are any areas of specific concern, it may be time to seek the help of a professional. That could mean anything from an Energy Worker/Reiki practitioner, a Life Coach, a Therapist, a Naturopath and/or a Chiropractor to get you aligned. If you feel that it is something more critical that needs addressing, speak to your primary care physician, nurse practitioner, psychologist or psychiatrist. There is nothing wrong with asking for and getting help. You are important and you're worth it. Remember, _"Our bodies are a source of truth, sometimes the truth hurts and we need help."_

Sole GLOW, Get Up and Go

Genetic history and family of origin influences have an effect on who you are no matter what. To some extent it is easy to identify some of the good stuff and some of the not-so-good stuff handed down in genes, including potential to have serious diseases. Especially those that tend to develop later in life, due to genetic factors. Family history contributions include the age-old argument about nature versus nurture in development, environmental factors and learned behaviors as we've discussed throughout this workbook.

The cultural considerations that should be considered when getting clear about this aspect of wellness are many and varied. The Black Womxn's BodyMind comes from so many combinations of cultures across the globe, that it's nearly impossible to lay out the combinations without having a DNA analysis to even start looking. One example of a physical issue is Black Womxn who are unable to walk a mile. It is a problem that is also affecting how our children are able to participate in normal physical activities. As adults, a sedentary lifestyle that looks like watching television way more than doing anything physical. If you think that's all you need you're trying to trick yourself, not me. Genetically, if someone is predisposed to being too heavy, having heart attacks at younger ages, or has a family history of more virulent cancers, their ability to manage wellness is also affected by what they do on a daily basis.

Now that we are the subject of moving our bodies, let's talk about **grounding** from the point of our thighs, legs and feet. As discussed earlier, the portion of the body governed by the Root / 1st Chakra are those two limbs that keep us moving. This includes those of you whose legs are on wheels. The physical problems associated with the legs include: cramps, clots (circulation, i.e. Deep Vein Thrombosis and Varicose Veins), weak ankles/heel pain, plantar fasciitis, bunions and even ingrown toenails.

I had both of my knees replaced a few years ago and stayed in the hospital for 2.5 weeks. I remember feeling so vulnerable and super sad one night *shhh... it's a secret** I got my night nurse to act as though my husband left and had him climb in the hospital bed with me, just so I could lay on his chest and actually get some sleep. I cried that night from feeling so grounded, safe and relieved. It was the best sleep I've ever had in the hospital to this day.

Considering the questions from the previous section, can you see how this area affects how you process this bodymind material? Take some time to meditate on these questions. I'll bet there are some things that you have given some thought to before reading this workbook. It's time to spend time on some answers. In the meantime...What can you do about this? The only exercise that I can really recommend for your legs is walking. Walking is excellent for cardio health, circulation, fitness, wellness and stress relief. If you're not allowed to do this, you already know your alternatives. For those with wheels, I know that the bicycles can be prejudicial but if you can get a hold of a hand cycle, you will get many of the same benefits. Other grounding exercises include yoga poses such as Goddess, Warrior I and II, Mountain, Chair and Child poses.

Physically supporting your grounding can be anything from improving your eating habits, engaging with a dietician, and embracing one of the vegetarian cookbook recipes you've been thinking about trying. You could also try soaking your feet regularly, not like washing in the shower, but placing a bowl of warm water and a rose oil for soaking your feet. Hey, if you're just watching tv, you might as well get some grounding out of it.

What to Feed the Your Hungry Roots

The foods that we eat affect our bodies in many ways. We don't eat just to feed hunger; it's necessary for vitamins, nutrients, proteins and all that jazz. We've heard the slogans "you are what you eat" a thousand times. Yet and still, we make choices that do not make our bodies feel good. They do nothing to get or keep us healthy, but they can make you feel comforted, can't they? If you're thinking that you don't have the will to make changes, you won't. However, if you have the thought that maybe some change is necessary, let's see what kinds of things we could add to our intake. Especially foods, vitamins and minerals that support our Root Chakra.

Nutritionists recommend the following foods that just happen to be red, and meet the purposes of this workbook:

- *Beets, Radishes, Red apples, Red cabbage, Strawberries, Dragon Fruit and Pomegranate*

- Foods that have roots like *Carrots, Sweet Potatoes, Parsnips, Lentils and Beans*
- Earthy foods that have high protein levels like *nuts* and, if you can eat them, *eggs*
- Other foods like *almond and peanut butter* (as long as you're not allergic)
- Lastly *hemp seeds, pumpkin seeds and chia seeds* because... seeds

I'm sure there are more foods to add to this list, but for now, just try to add a few at a time. It may not be the food for you to go crazy over and that's okay. Trying new foods is a good thing and eating more of what's good for you is even better. Your BodyMind will thank you for it. Promise.

These Feet were made for Walking into the Future

It's the final stretch of this journey to *Living a life you love and Loving the life you live!* Looking back on this trip we've taken together should feel like a major accomplishment in having a greater understanding of your bodymind, your love and your life. If you have unearthed questions that need answers, I hope that you are able to take the steps needed to get answers with your head held high. It is my sincere wish that you are able to pass this learning on to others in your life. Sisters, mothers, daughters, cousins and friends who you think need to spend some time on a walk with themselves.

Caring for your feet is so important. One thing can be said of those who take the time to care for their feet and that is that they likely take better care of themselves than those who do not. Those who are willing to wash the feet of others truly understand honoring another person and, when doing so, exhibit great strength in humbling themselves. Think of the spiritual practices you may know that include the washing of others feet. It is one of the most genuine ways that you can set your ego aside and show deference and respect to someone else.

Spending this last section on the feet seems like the exact right thing to me. I am often reminded that taking care of oneself includes taking care of your feet. For many Black Womxn, it is a ritual to get a pedicure. Whether it's self love or beautification doesn't matter. It's the process of soaking and massaging that makes the difference.

This tradition goes back as far as Ancient Egypt (Khemet, 2330 BCE) and has been passed down through the ages in one form or another. This ancient medicine is practiced as Reflexology today.

The purpose for this practice isn't just for beautification, it's a practice of treating the bodymind holistically. Imagine that the entire body is mapped out on the feet;every organ, bone and orifice from the sinuses to the stomach and the sacrum. Reflexology is similarly mapped out on the hands and ears, and would be included in a Reflexology session. The theory of this practice is that the body's corresponding areas are found in the sensitivities of the feet. Considering the theme of this book and my guiding principle that *"Our bodies are a source of truth, sometimes the truth hurts and we need help"* we must also consider the mental/emotional memories or physical experiences that may be stored here.

I recall having a reflexology session a week or two prior to finding out that I was pregnant with my first child. During this session, the Reflexologist was working the areas around my ankle (which corresponds to the uterus) and it was so painful and sensitive. My cycle was not yet late at that time, so I chalked it up to potentially relieving forthcoming menstrual cramps. Little did I know a tiny little zygote had started growing into my baby girl. It was from that point moving forward, I always checked my ankles to see if they were sensitive, swollen or indicating another concern. It was through this checking that I asked my gynecologist about potential problems and they couldn't find anything. Several years later I had a serious bout with ovarian cysts, and those that ruptured sent me to the hospital. Sometimes we get to know ourselves better than a medical test can show. Just know that while you may not be able to prove a problem, you can certainly do something to combat potential issues with food, vitamins, exercise and staying vigilant if anything changes.

Another thing about the feet that helps define the bodymind connection is how it connects to 'grounding' yourself. Here are just a few questions you can reflect on:

1. How do you carry yourself (move about the world) including "dragging your feet" or are you "light on your feet"?

2. How do you stand in your own personal power (where do you stand on things) seen in "standing up for the truth" or "standing your ground"? Or do simply go with "whatever"?

3. How do you walk/run towards people, places or things meant for or are good for you?

4. How do you walk or run away from people, places or things that have never, or no longer, serve(d) you?

It is my hope that these questions can lead you down a path to a greater understanding, not in comparison to others, but for your own sake. It is my sincere wish that you understand that your BodyMind can make you think, say or do things based on past experiences that have nothing to do with who you are today. As I've stated several times throughout this workbook, it is my desire to see you *"Live a life you love and Love the life you live!"*

ACKNOWLEDGMENTS

The devastating diagnosis of Autoimmune Rheumatoid Disease (RA) was actually somewhat of a relief, compared to the agony that I was in prior to the diagnosis. Becoming a patient requiring traditional medical interventions, while still believing that natural therapies work best was a true learning curve. I had lived my life without having medicine in my medicine cabinet. You would only find herbs, homeopathic medicine or tinctures. Everything changed just as I hit 40 and completed my 1st and only triathlon because within 6 months of that birthday I could barely stand up, let alone walk. This past decade has taught me so much more than what I knew to be true, just as I reached my 50th birthday. There's always room for growth, even when you're not looking to do just that.

There are so many people that have contributed to the completion of this very special self-love memoir/workbook. Those who contributed to my ability to get this done come from the experiences I've had, teachers of all kinds, books that I have read and contributed to, research articles I read for the one I published, people who I've talked to as a teacher and speaker, clients who have confided in me, and so much more.

I have the best family that a womxn could ask for and so I'd first like to acknowledge the unwavering support of my younger sister Nyne, who has not only financially supported me through difficult times, but fed me when everything in my life seemed to fall apart. She is my rock. My older sister, Seven, who helped me be the woman I am and has always been the one to encourage me to be her unapologetically. She has been the greatest example of my understanding that "this too, shall pass" in good times and bad. To roll with the punches and get up the next day to face the world head on. My older brother Kevin, is one of the 2 smartest men that I personally know (my dad being the other). He is the genius that inspired me to speak with good diction and learn for the sake of learning, not because I needed to pass some test. He used to read the dictionary for fun and expanded my vocabulary more than St. Monica's Elementary School could have ever possibly taught me. He amazes me with his masterful grasp on economics, politics and government. I told him to finish writing his book because the world needs to know what he has to say. That or get back to his incredible artistic talents. I relentlessly threaten him, just ask.

I have a very large extended family that has supported me in so many ways. Beyond the fact that my amazing, inspiring, loving uncles and aunts are some of the greatest people I know and love dearly. My cousins are just as incredible and some are my closest friends. There's too many to name them all, but I have to give these Sydnor daughters (Sandra, Debbie, Sheila, Bonnie, Rhonnie and Lynn) a major shout out because not only do they love me unconditionally, they respect me enough to ask for my thoughts, opinion, or assistance as a professional.

The Wyatt granddaughters (Toye, Suni and Robin) are a trio of the strongest women I know. Feisty, filled with ingenuity and integrity. All of them are what I call 'Black Womxn Brilliance' personified.

I have been lucky enough to have collected friends from everywhere I've lived or visited. My best friends are a few women, in particular, that I consider a part of my heart. Angela, who has been my friend since we were both 'knee-high to a grasshopper'; Yolanda, I've known since grade school, bonded with in high school, co-wrote a book together (Dear Yvette; Shattered Fairytales), and share secrets we'll both take to our grave; and Zakia, who never ceases to amaze me with her determination to get things done that she set out to do including writing her own book (#Alldone).

Other very close friends have special places in my heart because their hearts beat to the same drum as mine, in no particular order: Nichole, Bonnie, Christina, Stephanie, Freedom, Janice, Jasara-Joi, Twanna, Joannie, Londyn, Monique, Jessica, Sarah, Asia and Kebe have given me time, attention, memories, unforgettable vacations and invaluable companionship over many decades and many hard days throughout my diagnosis and treatment. I can only hope to be as good a friend to them as they have been to me.

My sisters in the struggles of RA have become my go-to for sharing what we know, opinions we may have, and simply enjoying the company of someone who really "gets" what it means to have Autoimmune Rheumatoid Disease (RA). Chantelle and Shantana (#iamSisterGirl) are my Rock Star SiStars. They are just two of whom this book is written for, but they're my favorites.

If I did not mention your name, charge it to my head and not my heart. Everyone who I've come into contact with has either given me something to think about and/or learn something new. I am in a constant state of growth, change, and wonder. I will explore all the things that I can think of and those that I haven't. Thank you for going on this journey with me! I love you!

RECOMMENDED READING LIST

Sisters of the Yam; Black women and self-recovery by bell hooks

Change Power: 37 Secrets to habit change success by Meg Selig

The Body Keeps the Score by Bessel Van Der Kolk

Discovering the Body's Wisdom by Mirka Knaster

You Can Heal Your Life by Louise Hay

Anatomy of the Spirit by Carolyn Myss

Psychology of the Body by Elliot Greene and Barbara Goodrich-Dun

African Holistic Health by Lailah O. Afrika

The Mindful Path to Self-Compassion by Christopher Germer

Eastern Body, Western Mind: Psychology.. the Chakra System Path.. Self by Anodea Judith

Made in the USA
Middletown, DE
18 June 2024

55986994R00070